JESUS, OUR LORD

Bible Study Guide

From the Bible-teaching ministry of

CHARLES R. SWINDOLL

INSIGHT FOR LIVING

Chuck graduated in 1963 from Dallas Theological Seminary, where he now serves as the school's fourth president, helping to prepare a new generation of men and women for the ministry. Chuck has served in pastorates in three states: Massachusetts, Texas, and California, including almost twenty-three years at the First Evangelical Free Church in Fullerton, California. His sermon messages have been aired over radio since 1979 as the "Insight for Living" broadcast. A best-selling author, Chuck has written numerous books and booklets on many subjects.

Based on the outlines and transcripts of Chuck's sermons, the study guide text is co-authored by Ken Gire, a graduate of Texas Christian University and Dallas Theological Seminary. He also wrote the Living Insights sections.

Editor in Chief: Cynthia Swindoll	**Publishing System Specialist:** Bob Haskins
Coauthor of Text: Ken Gire	**Director, Communications and Marketing Division:** Deedee Snyder
Author of Living Insights: Ken Gire	**Marketing Manager:** Alene Cooper
Assistant Editor: Wendy Peterson	**Project Coodinator:** Colette Muse
Copy Editors: Cheryl Gilmore Glenda Schlahta	**Production Manager:** John Norton
Designer: Gary Lett	**Printer:** Sinclair Printing Company

Unless otherwise identified, all Scripture references are from the New American Standard Bible, © The Lockman Foundation 1960, 1962, 1963, 1968, 1971, 1972, 1973, 1975, 1977. Used by permission.

The other translation cited is J. B. Phillips: The New Testament in Modern English [PHILLIPS].

An effort has been made to locate sources and obtain permission where necessary for the quotations used in this book. In the event of any unintentional omission, a modification will gladly be incorporated in future printings.

ISBN 0-8499-8584-6
COVER DESIGN: Nina Paris
COVER PHOTOGRAPHY: Robert Nease
COVER PAINTING: *Thomas the Doubter* by Carl Bloch
Printed in the United States of America

CONTENTS

INTRODUCTION

Jesus.

There is no greater name. He alone deserves our deepest reverence, our highest praise, our constant devotion, our daily obedience. Why? Because He *alone* is *Lord*.

These studies will turn our attention to Him. If you examine the table of contents, you will discover that one study follows another, tracing Christ's life in chronological order. So, we will be journeying through the New Testament with our Lord from His preexistence with the Father to His return to heaven as the ascended Christ.

In a day when the person of Christ is under such relentless attack by religious cults and secular philosophies, it's necessary that we who are Christians understand what the Bible declares and what it means when it mentions our following Jesus as our Lord.

May each study assist you in making that understanding a reality in your life.

Chuck Swindoll

Chuck Swindoll

PUTTING TRUTH INTO ACTION

Knowledge apart from application falls short of God's desire for His children. He wants us to apply what we learn so that we will change and grow. This study guide was prepared with these goals in mind. As you go through the following pages, we hope your desire to discover biblical truth will grow as your understanding of God's Word increases and that you will be encouraged to apply what you've learned.

To assist you in your study, we've included a section called Living Insights at the end of each lesson. These exercises will challenge you to study further and to think of specific ways to put your discoveries into action.

There are many ways to use this guide—in personal devotions, group studies, discussions with friends and family, and Sunday school classes. And, of course, it's an ideal study aid when you're listening to its corresponding "Insight for Living" radio series.

To benefit most from this study guide, we would encourage you to consider it a spiritual journal. That's why we've included space in the Living Insights for recording your thoughts and discoveries. We hope you'll return to those sections often for review and encouragement as you continue to grow in your walk with Christ.

Ken Gire

Ken Gire
Coauthor

JESUS, OUR LORD

Chapter 1

JESUS: HIS EXISTENCE BEFORE CREATION

Selected Scriptures

Clive Staples Lewis began his academic career at Oxford as a brilliant and confident young atheist. His anger at a God he no longer believed existed most probably stemmed from the devastating childhood experience of watching his mother being ravaged by cancer. He prayed to God to heal her, but the words, he felt, fell on deaf and distant ears; for just before he turned ten, his mother died.

In the years that followed, Lewis dismissed the existence of a caring, loving God and relegated the Bible to storybook status. As a student, his atheism flowered in Oxford's soil. But slowly and certainly, God was uprooting him to shake him free. Lewis resisted, his roots tenaciously clinging, but the pull of God was relentless. In his book *Surprised by Joy*, Lewis gives a vivid account of the battle for his soul.

> I was like a man who has lost "merely a pawn" and never dreams that this (in that state of the game) means mate in a few moves.[1]

Going on to describe his anxiety caused by God's pursuit, he states, "The fox had been dislodged from Hegelian Wood and was now running in the open, 'with all the wo in the world,' bedraggled and weary, hounds barely a field behind."[2] He continues with another image, "And so the great Angler played His fish and I never

---

1. C. S. Lewis, *Surprised by Joy: The Shape of My Early Life* (New York, N.Y.: Harcourt Brace Jovanovich, 1955), p. 222.

2. Lewis, *Surprised by Joy*, p. 225.

dreamed that the hook was in my tongue."[3] Finally, God dipped His net: the fish was still fighting, but the contest was over.

> You must picture me alone in that room in Magdalen, night after night, feeling, whenever my mind lifted even for a second from my work, the steady, unrelenting approach of Him whom I so earnestly desired not to meet. That which I greatly feared had at last come upon me. In the Trinity Term of 1929 I gave in, and admitted that God was God, and knelt and prayed: perhaps, that night, the most dejected and reluctant convert in all England. I did not then see what is now the most shining and obvious thing; the Divine humility which will accept a convert even on such terms. The Prodigal Son at least walked home on his own feet. But who can duly adore that Love which will open the high gates to a prodigal who is brought in kicking, struggling, resentful, and darting his eyes in every direction for a chance of escape?[4]

On that reluctant night, Jesus became C. S. Lewis' Lord.

The Question of Jesus' Identity

Before we ever come into the family of God, we, like Lewis, must come to grips with the identity of Jesus in a personal, one-on-one encounter. Upon entering Caesarea Philippi, Jesus penetrated His disciples' thinking with a question that forced just such an encounter: "Who do people say that the Son of Man is?" (Matt. 16:13). That question echoes as loudly today as it did back then.

Who Is Jesus, According to People Today?

Some say He's a great human teacher . . . the founder of Christianity . . . a Nazarene carpenter's son . . . a Jew who claimed to be the Messiah . . . a first-century martyr who died for a noble cause . . . the Son of God. In his book *Mere Christianity*, Lewis narrows the options to three.

---

3. Lewis, *Surprised by Joy*, p. 211.
4. Lewis, *Surprised by Joy*, pp. 228–29.

I am trying here to prevent anyone saying the really foolish thing that people often say about Him: "I'm ready to accept Jesus as a great moral teacher, but I don't accept His claim to be God." That is the one thing we must not say. A man who was merely a man and said the sort of things Jesus said would not be a great moral teacher. He would either be a lunatic—on a level with the man who says he is a poached egg—or else he would be the Devil of Hell. You must make your choice. Either this man was, and is, the Son of God: or else a madman or something worse. You can shut Him up for a fool, you can spit at Him and kill Him as a demon; or you can fall at His feet and call Him Lord and God. But let us not come with any patronising nonsense about His being a great human teacher. He has not left that open to us. He did not intend to.[5]

Who Was Jesus, According to the People of the First Century?

Like an impoverished orphan, this question begged in the streets of Jerusalem. His disciples asked: "Who then is this, that even the wind and the sea obey Him?" (Mark 4:41). Reporting to Jesus the conclusions of others, His disciples said, "Some say John the Baptist; and others, Elijah; but still others, Jeremiah, or one of the prophets" (Matt. 16:14).

The scribes and Pharisees' applecart of messianic expectations was especially upset by this unsettling preacher from Nazareth: "Who is this man who speaks blasphemies?" (Luke 5:21); "Who is this man who even forgives sins?" (7:49). The persistent question went as far as to knock on the doors of the highest government officials. Herod pondered: "I myself had John beheaded; but who is this man about whom I hear such things?" (9:9). Finally and climactically—face-to-face—Pilate questioned Jesus' identity: "Are You the King of the Jews?" (23:3).

Who Is Jesus, According to His Own Claim?

After His disciples told Jesus who the people thought Him to

5. C. S. Lewis, *Mere Christianity*, rev. and enl. (1952; reprint, New York, N.Y.: Macmillan Publishing Co., 1960), pp. 40–41.

be, Jesus handed Peter the pointed end of the question.

> He said to them, "But who do *you* say that I am?"
> And Simon Peter answered and said, "Thou art the
> Christ, the Son of the living God." And Jesus an-
> swered and said to him, "Blessed are you, Simon
> Barjona, because flesh and blood did not reveal this
> to you, but My Father who is in heaven." (Matt.
> 16:15–17, emphasis added)

Jesus' blessing on Peter indicated that He agreed with and ap-
proved of Peter's statement. Another disciple, Thomas, gave a similar confession in John 20:26–29.

> And after eight days again His disciples were
> inside, and Thomas with them. Jesus came, the doors
> having been shut, and stood in their midst, and said,
> "Peace be with you." Then He said to Thomas,
> "Reach here your finger, and see My hands; and
> reach here your hand, and put it into My side; and
> be not unbelieving, but believing." Thomas an-
> swered and said to Him, "My Lord and my God!"
> Jesus said to him, "Because you have seen Me, have
> you believed? Blessed are they who did not see, and
> yet believed."

Notice that Jesus did not rebuke Thomas for calling Him God,
nor did He rebuke him for falling down to worship Him.[6]

The Issue of Jesus' Eternality

Turning to John 8, we can almost feel the heat rising from the
page as the conflict between Jesus and the Pharisees intensified.

According to Jesus Himself

Even at a distance we can hear the clash of sharp words wielded
in fury. As we come closer, we can see the sparks flying from a
debate over Jesus' identity.

---

6. Compare Paul and Barnabas' response to the crowd's adulation after they healed a lame
man in Acts 14:8–15. Even angels refuse human worship (see Rev. 22:8–9). When Thomas
fell down to worship Christ, however, no such rebuke was given. The worship was accepted.

They answered and said to Him, "Abraham is our father." Jesus said to them, "If you are Abraham's children, do the deeds of Abraham. But as it is, you are seeking to kill Me, a man who has told you the truth, which I heard from God; this Abraham did not do. You are doing the deeds of your father." They said to Him, "We were not born of fornication; we have one Father, even God." Jesus said to them, "If God were your Father, you would love Me; for I proceeded forth and have come from God, for I have not even come on My own initiative, but He sent Me. Why do you not understand what I am saying? It is because you cannot hear My word." (vv. 39–43)

In the following verses, the jabs became more violent. Jesus lunged for the heart, "You are of your father the devil" (v. 44), and the Pharisees parried a rapier reply, "You are a Samaritan and have a demon" (v. 48). Undaunted, Jesus stood His ground: "If anyone keeps My word he shall never see death" (v. 51). With these words, the Pharisees' attack became even more furious.

The Jews said to Him, "Now we know that You have a demon. Abraham died, and the prophets also; and You say, 'If anyone keeps My word, he shall never taste of death.' Surely You are not greater than our father Abraham, who died? The prophets died too; whom do You make Yourself out to be?" Jesus answered, . . . "Your father Abraham rejoiced to see My day, and he saw it and was glad." The Jews therefore said to Him, "You are not yet fifty years old, and have You seen Abraham?" (vv. 52–54, 56–57)

Jesus then disarmed his aggressors with a claim that, to them, was not only bold and brash but blasphemous as well.

Jesus said to them, "Truly, truly, I say to you, before Abraham was born, I am." (v. 58)[7]

When Jesus referred to Himself as "I am," He was not only

---

7. Three times in John 8 "I am" is used in the absolute sense (vv. 24, 28, 58). In none of these passages does the third personal pronoun "he" follow the "I am" in the Greek text.

asserting His supremacy over Abraham and over time, but He was also asserting His identity with God.[8] And this the outraged Pharisees perceived as blasphemy. C. S. Lewis helps convey how stunning Jesus' words were.

> Among these Jews there suddenly turns up a man who goes about talking as if He was God. . . . He says He has always existed. . . . Among Pantheists . . . anyone might say that he was a part of God, or one with God: there would be nothing very odd about it. But this man, since He was a Jew, could not mean that kind of God. God, in their language, meant the Being outside the world Who had made it and was infinitely different from anything else. And when you have grasped that, you will see that what this man said was, quite simply, the most shocking thing that has ever been uttered by human lips.[9]

So shocking was this assertion that the Pharisees

> picked up stones to throw at Him; but Jesus hid Himself, and went out of the temple. (v. 59)

According to the Law, blasphemy against God's name warranted death by stoning (Lev. 24:16). Later, in John 10, the Jews again took up stones to kill Jesus for the same reason:

> The Jews answered Him, "For a good work we do not stone You, but for blasphemy; and because You, being a man, make Yourself out to be God." (v. 33)

According to John's Gospel

The eternality of Christ is asserted not only by Jesus Himself but also by His closest disciple—the disciple whom Christ loved—John.

> In the beginning was the Word, and the Word was with God, and the Word was God. (1:1)

---

8. When God commissioned Moses as His spokesman and leader of His people, Moses asked how he should reply if the people questioned him regarding the identity of the One who sent him. God's response was this: "And God said to Moses, 'I AM WHO I AM'; and He said, 'Thus you shall say to the sons of Israel, "I AM has sent me to you"'" (Exod. 3:14).

9. Lewis, *Mere Christianity*, p. 40.

The identity of this *Word* is revealed in verses 14–18.

> And the Word became flesh, and dwelt among us, and we beheld His glory, glory as of the only begotten from the Father, full of grace and truth. John bore witness of Him, and cried out, saying, "This was He of whom I said, 'He who comes after me has a higher rank than I, for He existed before me.'" For of His fulness we have all received, and grace upon grace. For the Law was given through Moses; grace and truth were realized through Jesus Christ. No man has seen God at any time; the only begotten God, who is in the bosom of the Father, He has explained Him.

The *Word* is Jesus Christ. Like a translator teaching someone a foreign language, Jesus explained God to us, translating Him into words we could understand. Jesus could do this because He was not only with God, He was God.[10]

According to Paul's Letters

In Philippians 2:5–7, Paul affirms John's teaching about Christ's deity and incarnation.

> Have this attitude in yourselves which was also in Christ Jesus, who, although He existed in the form of God, did not regard equality with God a thing to be grasped, but emptied Himself, taking the form of a bond-servant, and being made in the likeness of men.

In another letter, Paul again agrees with John—that Jesus not only existed before creation but that "all things came into being by Him, and apart from Him nothing came into being that has come into being" (John 1:3).

> For by Him all things were created, both in the heavens and on earth, visible and invisible, whether thrones or dominions or rulers or authorities—all

---

10. The Greek word translated *with* means "face-to-face." "Probably we should understand from the preposition the two ideas of accompaniment and relationship. . . . Not only did the Word exist 'in the beginning', but He existed in the closest possible connection with the Father." Leon Morris, *The Gospel According to John* (Grand Rapids, Mich.: William B. Eerdmans Publishing Co., 1971), p. 76.

things have been created by Him and for Him. And He is before all things, and in Him all things hold together. (Col. 1:16–17)

A chapter later, Paul echoes this thought.

See to it that no one takes you captive through philosophy and empty deception, according to the tradition of men, according to the elementary principles of the world, rather than according to Christ. For in Him all the fulness of Deity dwells in bodily form. (2:8–9)

The Importance of Jesus' Deity

The deity of Jesus is important on two levels, theological and practical.

Theologically, if Jesus isn't eternally God, then the credibility of all of Scripture is undermined. If these sections that assert Jesus' preexistence and divinity are not true, then what in the Bible is true? If some parts of Scripture are faulty, how do we know whether the rest isn't faulty too? This issue wouldn't be some slight bend in the road of Christianity—it would be a dead end.

And practically, if Jesus is a mere man, our faith is empty and our hope vanishes. We couldn't turn to Him for help, either for salvation from our sins or for salvation from our day-to-day struggles, because He would have only the same power and resources that we have.

So much depends on who we recognize Christ to be. In the depths of your heart, who do you say He is?

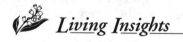 *Living Insights*

Boiled down to the basics, the essence of life can be distilled into one question: "But who do you say that I am?" (Matt. 16:15). Let's examine this question and follow it to its logical conclusions with the help of the chart on the following page.

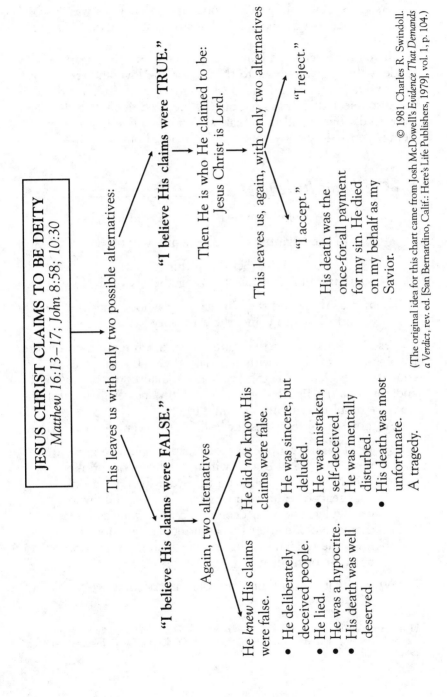

JESUS CHRIST CLAIMS TO BE DEITY
Matthew 16:13–17; John 8:58; 10:30

This leaves us with only two possible alternatives:

"I believe His claims were FALSE."

Again, two alternatives

He *knew* His claims were false.

- He deliberately deceived people.
- He lied.
- He was a hypocrite.
- His death was well deserved.

He did *not* know His claims were false.

- He was sincere, but deluded.
- He was mistaken, self-deceived.
- He was mentally disturbed.
- His death was most unfortunate. A tragedy.

"I believe His claims were TRUE."

Then He is who He claimed to be: Jesus Christ is Lord.

This leaves us, again, with only two alternatives

"I accept."

His death was the once-for-all payment for my sin. He died on my behalf as my Savior.

"I reject."

© 1981 Charles R. Swindoll.

(The original idea for this chart came from Josh McDowell's *Evidence That Demands a Verdict*, rev. ed. [San Bernardino, Calif.: Here's Life Publishers, 1979], vol. 1, p. 104.)

9

As C. S. Lewis showed us, concluding that Jesus was "a good moral teacher" is not an option. Jesus is either lunatic, liar, or He is Lord.

If you have accepted Him as Lord, then your time spent in this guide will bring you closer to the Savior you love and serve.

And if you haven't decided who Jesus is, or if you have decided but also rejected Him as Lord of your life, let this study be an open door to discovery and reevaluation. You may, like Lewis, wind up being surprised by a joy you've only dreamed of.

 *Living Insights*

"Before Abraham was born, I am." (John 8:58)

In the beginning was the Word. (John 1:1)

He is before all things,
and in Him all things hold together. (Col. 1:17)

"I am the Alpha and the Omega . . . who is and who was and who is to come, the Almighty." (Rev. 1:8)

Jesus' preexistent, eternal nature is so much more than remote theology, out of touch with our daily lives. It assures us of His equality with God the Father, validates the authority of His words, and confirms the limitlessness of His divine power. It is the hope we have of all His promises coming true.

Author Ken Gire brings the reality of it even closer to home:

> There is no one else qualified to grant forgiveness. No one else who will never leave or forsake you. No one else who can heal your diseases or dry your tears or calm your anxieties. No one else who can understand your deepest secret or your darkest shame. No one else who can bring back the joy, the love, the tenderness that has been stolen from you by abuse or neglect.[11]

What situations or hurts in your life need the reminder of

---

11. From the study guide *Issues and Answers in Jesus' Day*, coauthored by Ken Gire, from the Bible-teaching ministry of Charles R. Swindoll (Fullerton, Calif.: Insight for Living, 1990), p. 6.

Christ's eternal qualifications to handle them?

_____

_____

_____

What particular strength of Christ's do you need to meet the most challenging of these areas?

_____

_____

Won't you take your requests to Him now? His love and compassion are as everlasting as He is, and He longs to relieve you of the burdens that weigh your heart down (1 Pet. 5:7).

Chapter 2
JESUS: A BIRTH LIKE NONE OTHER
Luke 1:26–35; Matthew 1:18–25

It would be a royal birth—a birth like none other. Everybody who was anybody would be there, national and international dignitaries alike. It would be the major media event in history. Every network and every newspaper would cover it.

Of course, the royal family would receive the ultimate in VIP treatment: a Rolls Royce limousine for transportation, the Presidential Suite at the finest hotel. For the baby, the most beautiful bassinet money could buy. Satin sheets. A royal wardrobe. The highest quality staff of servants available in the world to attend to the young heir's every coo and cry.

Certainly all the world would stop in reverence for the royal baby's arrival. Shops would close. Factories would shut down. All transportation and commerce would cease. Every heart would eagerly await this great and glorious birth.

At least, that's how we would have expected the scenario to read. However, the scenario God arranged for the royal birth of His Son reads strangely different. In the last stage of Mary's pregnancy, the royal family traveled eighty-five miles to Bethlehem to be counted in the national census. In that small city, swollen from the influx of travelers, there was no room for the expectant couple. The inns were packed; the only available accommodation was a stable crowded with the animals of the inn's guests.

In the stable, a feeding trough made do for a crib. Hay served as both mattress and sheets for the young king. Rags used to wipe down the animals were the infant's clothes. Sheep, donkeys, and furtive barn mice were the heir's only attendants. A barnyard stench hung heavy in the air. The stable was dark and dirty—a disquieting place for a woman in the throes of childbirth. Far from home. Far from family. Far from what she expected for her firstborn. Except for Joseph, there was no one to share her pain; no one to share her joy. Yes, there were angels announcing His arrival—but only to a lowly band of blue-collar shepherds.

And thus, in the little town of Bethlehem . . . that one silent night . . . the royal birth of God's only Son tiptoed quietly by . . . as the world slept.

The Centrality of Jesus Christ

Without Jesus in the manger, there is no Christianity. Apart from Christ, Christianity is an empty feeding trough, only so much wood and straw. For Jesus Christ and Christianity are really one and the same, and Christians—those called by Christ's name—are people who are personally, individually related to *Him*. The baby Jesus is the central focus not only in our nativity scenes but also in our lives.

However, just as it's easy to lose the simplicity and purity of Christmas amid the ribbons and bows of the holidays, so it's easy to lose our devotion to Christ amid the tinsel and glitter of life. Paul warns of this danger in 2 Corinthians 11:3:

> But I am afraid, lest as the serpent deceived Eve by
> his craftiness, your minds should be led astray from
> the simplicity and purity of devotion to Christ.

J. B. Phillips is even more descriptive in his rendering of this verse: "I am afraid that your minds may be seduced from a single-hearted devotion to him."

Single-heartedness, simplicity, purity of devotion to Christ—these are our basics. What blocking and tackling are to football, keeping your eye on the ball is to baseball, and not giving up the baseline is to basketball, so devotion to Christ is to our Christian life.

Oftentimes, when athletes are having trouble with their game, it's because they've gotten away from the basics. We're a lot like that spiritually—we wander away so easily from the pure and the simple.

How about you? Are you still purely and simply devoted to Christ—like Martha's sister, Mary, who sat attentively at Jesus' feet (Luke 10:39–42)? Or have you been led astray by distractions—like Martha in the kitchen (vv. 40–41)? What about your Christian life? Are you knowing more now but enjoying it less? Maybe you need to get back to the basics—pure, single-hearted devotion to Christ.

The Superiority of Jesus Christ

Not only is Christ central, He is superior to everything in heaven and on earth. He was no ordinary man; He was God. His birth was no ordinary birth; it was a sinless arrival.

His Divine Nature

We have to remember, when we think of Jesus' birth, that there was never a time when He did not exist. Before Abraham was, Jesus was (John 8:58); before the earth was created, Jesus existed (1:1). Jesus is superior to all because He is Creator of all (v. 3). Jesus—the same yesterday, today, and forever (Heb. 13:8)—was, is, and forever will be God.

His Virgin Birth

How could God, then, become human yet remain uninfected by humanity's sinfulness? After all, a sinful savior couldn't really be a savior if he were just as contaminated as we are. His birth and life would have to be unique.

1. *Possibilities at the Father's disposal.* As a first option, God could have chosen for Jesus to have been born of a good human father and mother. However, as David describes, there is an inescapable dilemma inherent in natural conception.

> Behold, I was brought forth in iniquity,
> And in sin my mother conceived me. (Ps. 51:5)

And again in Psalm 58:3.

> The wicked are estranged from the womb;
> These who speak lies go astray from birth.

An echo of this truth surfaces in Romans 5:12.

> Therefore, just as through one man sin entered into
> the world, and death through sin, and so death
> spread to all men, because all sinned.

In this option, Jesus would have been all humanity—unavoidably sinful—and no deity.

As a second option, God could have chosen His Son to be created, like an angel, having neither father nor mother. As a created being, He would have been preserved from sin's contamination. In this case, however, He would have been all deity and no humanity. He could not have been a savior, because a savior must be a perfect representative of both heaven and earth, of both God and humanity.

As a third option, God could have chosen to incarnate the spirit of Christ in a human body, not unlike what is commonly referred to as reincarnation. The problem with this option is that He would not have been fully human in a technical sense. Scripture tells us Jesus had His own body, "a body Thou hast prepared for Me" (Heb. 10:5). If Christ's spirit had been simply deposited into the body of another, it would not have been His own—not His own heart, not His own personality, not His own birth that would fulfill prophecy.

As a final option, God could have chosen to select a virgin who, through miraculous conception, could give birth to a child both fully human and fully divine. And this is just what He did, as the multiple testimonies in Scripture attest.

2. *Actuality, according to Scripture.* About eight hundred years before Christ's birth, Isaiah stood before King Ahaz and prophesied this special event, which would serve as a sign to the nation.

> "Therefore the Lord Himself will give you a sign:
> Behold, a virgin will be with child and bear a son,
> and she will call His name Immanuel." (Isa. 7:14)

In Hebrew the word for *virgin* meant simply "a young maiden."[1] But when the Hebrew Old Testament was translated into Greek, as the Septuagint, this word was given a much narrower meaning: "one who had not known another intimately."[2] The translators understood the miraculous nature of the passage, recognizing that a young woman giving birth to a son named Immanuel would hardly qualify as a sign. So their word choice reflected the uniqueness God intended to convey.

This same, more precise Greek word is also used in Luke 1. Luke's record is especially valuable because the facts have been investigated by a physician's thorough mind.

> Now in the sixth month the angel Gabriel was
> sent from God to a city in Galilee, called Nazareth,
> to a virgin engaged to a man whose name was Jo-
> seph, of the descendants of David; and the virgin's
> name was Mary. (vv. 26–27)

Twice in verse 27 the word *virgin* is used. But it is the broader context of the angel's conversation with Mary that determines its distinct meaning.

1. The Hebrew word is *almah*.
2. The Greek word is *parthenos*.

And coming in, he said to her, "Hail, favored one! The Lord is with you." But she was greatly troubled at this statement, and kept pondering what kind of salutation this might be. And the angel said to her, "Do not be afraid, Mary; for you have found favor with God. And behold, you will conceive in your womb, and bear a son, and you shall name Him Jesus. He will be great, and will be called the Son of the Most High; and the Lord God will give Him the throne of His father David; and He will reign over the house of Jacob forever; and His kingdom will have no end." (vv. 28–33)

Her response to this revelation determines the exact meaning of the Greek word translated *virgin*.

And Mary said to the angel, "How can this be, since I am a virgin?" (v. 34)

In this verse, she literally says, "I know not a man," rather than using the word *virgin*. The clear implication is that she had never known a man intimately, so it would be physically impossible for her to give birth to a child. In response, the angel describes the details of the miracle to her.

And the angel answered and said to her, "The Holy Spirit will come upon you, and the power of the Most High will overshadow you; and for that reason the holy offspring shall be called the Son of God." (v. 35)

Of course, critics may argue that she was only a virgin at the time of the angel's revelation and later had relations with Joseph that produced the child. However, Matthew 1:18 decisively refutes that theory.

Now the birth of Jesus Christ was as follows. When His mother Mary had been betrothed to Joseph, before they came together she was found to be with child by the Holy Spirit.

Matthew carefully notes that Mary was pregnant *before* she and Joseph came together. According to Jewish custom, the time of betrothal was a twelve-month period of engagement that was an official, binding commitment which could only be broken legally by divorce, or, in the case of unfaithfulness, by death from stoning. The betrothal arrangement was so binding that Joseph was already viewed as Mary's husband:

> And Joseph her husband, being a righteous man, and not wanting to disgrace her, desired to put her away secretly. (v. 19)

Joseph was stunned at the turn of events and found himself in a quandary between conviction and compassion. Interceding on Mary's behalf, however, an angel clarifies the situation to her confused husband.

> But when he had considered this, behold, an angel of the Lord appeared to him in a dream, saying, "Joseph, son of David, do not be afraid to take Mary as your wife; for that which has been conceived in her is of the Holy Spirit. And she will bear a Son; and you shall call His name Jesus, for it is He who will save His people from their sins." (vv. 20–21)

In the next two verses, Matthew comments on this miraculous event, citing it as the sign referred to in Isaiah 7:14.

> Now all this took place that what was spoken by the Lord through the prophet might be fulfilled, saying, "Behold, the virgin shall be with child, and shall bear a Son, and they shall call His name Immanuel," which translated means, "God with us." (Matthew 1:22–23)

And Matthew adds a happy postscript to the story:

> And Joseph arose from his sleep, and did as the angel of the Lord commanded him, and took her as his wife, and kept her a virgin until she gave birth to a Son; and he called His name Jesus. (vv. 24–25)

The Practicality of It All

The virgin birth has far-reaching ramifications of practical significance. Because Christianity *is* Christ, if Christ is only a man, then Christianity is only a human religion. And a man-made religion falls apart in at least three areas.

First, *a natural savior provides no supernatural help.* We need supernatural forgiveness because we have a lifetime of sins and regrets. We need supernatural peace because, try as we might through relaxation techniques, mind-numbing drugs, or pouring our energies into denial, we can't manufacture peace on our own. And we need the supernatural promise of eternal life because we are helpless in ourselves to conquer our greatest fear, death.

Second, *a strictly human savior offers no divine hope.* To borrow Longfellow's words, "life is but an empty dream"[3] if Christ is only a man. When we hurt, we'd get only a temporary hug. When we need forgiveness, we'd get only a condescending smile. We'd have no hope that is grounded in a reality bigger than our own.

And third, *a sinful savior is really no savior at all.* If your only hope of rescue is the person sinking in quicksand next to you, then you have no hope of rescue. A savior must be sinless, and we have just such a Savior in Christ because His birth was truly like none other.

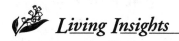 *Living Insights*

The virgin birth of Christ, like His preexistence, is more closely connected to our lives than we can perhaps realize. The truth of it guarantees supernatural help in our natural helplessness, divine hope in our mortal hopelessness. This mysterious mingling of uncompromised divinity and complete humanity makes Christ uniquely superior and therefore sufficient to meet our deepest needs.

Yes, we nod our heads in agreement, *this is all theologically correct and true.* But perhaps, if we're honest, it *is* more than we can realize, more than we can fathom. And perhaps that's why we don't often ponder its meaning. And, more than that, perhaps that's why we treat God's help as if it were human help, His hope as if it were a shimmering mirage that would fade if we looked at it too hard.

When you wrestle with circumstances or difficulties in relationships that are beyond your ability to resolve, do you seek God's supernatural help? How do you view His attitude toward the situation—as someone who will deliver you from all your fears

---

3. Henry Wadsworth Longfellow, from "A Psalm of Life," as quoted in *Bartlett's Familiar Quotations,* 15th ed., rev. and enl., ed. Emily Morison Beck (Boston, Mass.: Little, Brown and Co., 1980), p. 509.

(Ps. 34:4), or as someone who helps those who help themselves?[4] How does the truth of Hebrews 4:14–16 influence your thoughts?

_____

_____

_____

Are you afraid to hope for anything good from the Lord? Have you been so disappointed by the people in your life that you feel Christ won't be any different? How do His sinlessness and His inability to lie affect your perspective (see Heb. 6:17–20; Matt. 7:11)?

_____

_____

_____

Our supernatural Savior, conceived by the power of the Holy Spirit and born miraculously of a virgin, has given us His unchanging word that He is ready and willing to lavish the riches of His grace on us (see Eph. 1:7–8). Draw near to Him, and take His truth into your heart, won't you? As Paul wrote,

> I pray that the eyes of your heart may be enlightened, so that you may know what is the hope of His calling, what are the riches of the glory of His inheritance in the saints, and what is the surpassing greatness of His power toward us who believe. (vv. 18–19a)

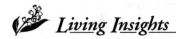 *Living Insights*   STUDY TWO

Sometimes our fears and our helpless, hopeless feelings come when we have drifted away from the power of Christ's presence— when He is out of the center of our lives. Like Martha, we start out with good intentions that are just a shade off, then we get more and more distracted, until the meaning of the moment is obliterated in a burst of exasperation.

---

4. This idea is found not in the Bible but in the writings of Benjamin Franklin.

If you need to recenter yourself in Christ—if you want to come out of Martha's hot kitchen and cool off at Jesus' feet with Mary—then we encourage you to find a quiet place and let this prayer based on Mary and Martha's story in Luke 10:38–42 help you get started.

Dear Savior at whose feet I now sit,

When you knock on the door to my heart, what is it you are looking for? What is it you want? Is it not to come in to dine with me? Is it not for fellowship?

And yet, so often, where do you find me? At your feet? No. In the kitchen. How many times have I become distracted and left you there . . . sitting . . . waiting . . . longing? . . .

Forgive me for being so much distracted by my preparations and so little attracted by your presence. For being so diligent in my duties and so negligent in my devotion. For being so quick to my feet and so slow to yours.

Help me to understand that it is an intimate moment you seek from me, not an elaborate meal.

Guard my heart this day from the many distractions that vie for my attention. And help me to fix my eyes on you. Not on my rank in the kingdom, as did the disciples. Not on the finer points of theology, as did the scribes. Not on the sins of others, as did the Pharisees. Not on a place of worship, as did the woman at the well. Not on the budget, as did Judas. But on you.

Bring me out of the kitchen, Lord. Bid me come to your feet. And there may I thrill to sit and adore you. . . .[5]

5. Ken Gire, Intimate Moments with the Savior (Grand Rapids, Mich.: Zondervan Publishing House, 1989), p. 69.

Chapter 3

JESUS: HIS GOD-MAN LIFESTYLE

Selected Scriptures

The Incarnation is what C. S. Lewis called "the Grand Miracle" of Christianity. It is "the central chapter" of a novel, upon which the whole plot turns.

> The story of the Incarnation is the story of a descent and resurrection. . . . I am talking of this whole, huge pattern of descent, down, down, and then up again. . . . The coming down, not only into humanity, but into those nine months which precede human birth, . . . and going lower still into being a corpse. . . . One has the picture of a diver, stripping off garment after garment, making himself naked, then flashing for a moment in the air, and then down through the green, and warm, and sunlit water into the pitch black, cold, freezing water, down into the mud and slime, then up again, his lungs almost bursting, back again to the green and warm and sunlit water, and then at last out into the sunshine, holding in his hand the dripping thing he went down to get. This thing is human nature; but, associated with it, all nature, the new universe.[1]

A Definition: The Meaning of the Incarnation

In simplest terms, the Incarnation is the union of God and humanity in the person of Jesus Christ. This union took place at the moment of conception, when both natures melded, inseparable yet unmixed (see Luke 1:31–35). In this mysterious union, undiminished deity was veiled in untainted humanity. Coequal, coeternal, and coexistent with the Father, Jesus was both fully God

---

1. C. S. Lewis, *God in the Dock: Essays on Theology and Ethics* (Grand Rapids, Mich.: William B. Eerdmans Publishing Co., 1970), p. 82.

and fully human.[2] In the Incarnation, God dived down into the depths of creation and became a man.[3]

> In the beginning was the Word, and the Word was with God, and the Word was God. . . .
> And the Word became flesh, and dwelt among us, and we beheld His glory, glory as of the only begotten from the Father, full of grace and truth. (John 1:1, 14; compare 2 Cor. 5:19)

An Explanation: Two Natures in One Person

The most beautiful and breathtaking nativity scene is found in Philippians 2:5-7:

> Have this attitude in yourselves which was also in Christ Jesus, who, although He existed in the form of God, did not regard equality with God a thing to be grasped, but emptied Himself, taking the form of a bond-servant, and being made in the likeness of men.

In this sacred scene, divine humility glows in the subdued light of the Incarnation, bathed in hues of another world. The Creator willingly submitted to the laws of the very universe He had created. He released independence and became dependent. He gave up being the One served to become the servant.

The God-Man as God

In emptying Himself (v. 7), the Son did not shed His deity; in becoming a man, He did not become something less than God. Rather, He voluntarily released His grasp on His divine prerogatives and set aside the independent use of His powers as deity.

The God-Man as Man

As a man, Jesus could do two things He was unable to do as God: be tempted by Satan and die. Hebrews 4:14-16 shows us how this affects our relationship to Him.

---

2. The root of the word *incarnation* means "flesh." Chile con *carne* is literally "chile with flesh" or "chili with meat." Incarnation is the act of becoming "in flesh" or embodied.

3. For more information, see L. Berkhof's *Systematic Theology*, 4th ed., rev. and enl. (Grand Rapids, Mich.: William B. Eerdmans Publishing Co., 1941), pp. 333-36.

Since then we have a great high priest who has passed through the heavens, Jesus the Son of God, let us hold fast our confession. For we do not have a high priest who cannot sympathize with our weaknesses, but one who has been tempted in all things as we are, yet without sin. Let us therefore draw near with confidence to the throne of grace, that we may receive mercy and may find grace to help in time of need.

We have a Savior who has been there—walked where we walk . . . hurt where we hurt . . . cried where we cry . . . ached where we ache. And so, when we come to Him in time of need, He does not scold us or shake His head in irritated disgust. He is sympathetic. When Jesus was cut, He bled; when He was sad, He wept; when He got hungry, His stomach gnawed within; when He got cold, He shivered; when He got hot, He sweated; when His heart stopped, He died.

Because He was human, He experienced our weakness—yet without ever succumbing to sin. He withstood the full fury of temptation: 100 percent of the agonizing attacks of Satan, the full measure of the tiring and emotionally wrenching ordeal. Because He suffered Satan's attacks to the end without giving in, He endured greater temptation than us—not less.

Some Illustrations: Both Natures Revealed Back-to-Back

Numerous eyewitnesses cite times when deity peeked through the drawn curtain of Jesus' humanity.

Matthew 14:22–33

In verses 22–23, Jesus shows His humanity through His dependence on the Father in prayer.

And immediately He made the disciples get into the boat, and go ahead of Him to the other side, while He sent the multitudes away. And after He had sent the multitudes away, He went up to the mountain by Himself to pray; and when it was evening, He was there alone.

In verses 24–27, He demonstrates His deity by walking on the water.

But the boat was already many stadia away from the land, battered by the waves; for the wind was contrary. And in the fourth watch of the night He came to them, walking on the sea. And when the disciples saw Him walking on the sea, they were frightened, saying, "It is a ghost!" And they cried out for fear. But immediately Jesus spoke to them, saying, "Take courage, it is I; do not be afraid."

This unveiling of deity resulted in the disciples' worship of Jesus and a confession of belief (vv. 28–33).

Luke 8:22–25

In a scene similar to the one in Matthew, we see Jesus on the sea again, this time weary and needing rest.

Now it came about on one of those days, that He and His disciples got into a boat, and He said to them, "Let us go over to the other side of the lake." And they launched out. But as they were sailing along He fell asleep; and a fierce gale of wind descended upon the lake, and they began to be swamped and to be in danger. And they came to Him and woke Him up, saying, "Master, Master, we are perishing!" And being aroused, He rebuked the wind and the surging waves, and they stopped, and it became calm. And He said to them, "Where is your faith?" And they were fearful and amazed, saying to one another, "Who then is this, that He commands even the winds and the water, and they obey Him?"

The humanity of Christ can be seen in the deep sleep He had succumbed to, while His deity is clearly shown in His commanding power over the wind and waves.

John 11:32–36, 41–46

Jesus had often gone to Bethany to rest and refresh Himself among the family of Mary, Martha, and Lazarus. On this occasion, however, we see the Savior in grief and unrest.

Therefore, when Mary came where Jesus was, she saw Him, and fell at His feet, saying to Him, "Lord, if You had been here, my brother would not have died." When Jesus therefore saw her weeping, and the Jews who came with her, also weeping, He was deeply moved in spirit, and was troubled, and said, "Where have you laid him?" They said to Him, "Lord, come and see." Jesus wept. And so the Jews were saying, "Behold how He loved him!" (vv. 32–36)

In the shortest, but one of the most profoundly penetrating verses of Scripture—"Jesus wept"—the humanity of Jesus pours from the page. At the tomb of Lazarus, a gamut of emotions ran through Him: He "was deeply moved" and "was troubled" and finally "wept." But back-to-back with this unguarded display of humanity we see the deity of Christ stand tall and resolute in verses 41–44, when He raised Lazarus from the dead.

And so they removed the stone. And Jesus raised His eyes, and said, "Father, I thank Thee that Thou heardest Me. And I knew that Thou hearest me always; but because of the people standing around I said it, that they may believe that Thou didst send Me." And when He had said these things, He cried out with a loud voice, "Lazarus, come forth." He who had died came forth, bound hand and foot with wrappings; and his face was wrapped around with a cloth. Jesus said to them, "Unbind him, and let him go."

Practical Results: How Both Bring Benefit

The union of deity and humanity in the person of Christ is referred to in theological circles as the hypostatic union. As dry and static as that may sound, this doctrine is not a dusty piece of academic trivia. It is both vibrant and vital to our experience of the Christian life. Because Jesus is God, He is able to authentically forgive sins (Mark 2:7), to understand our deepest needs and weaknesses (Heb. 2:17; 4:15), and to be a mediator between God and man (Gal. 3:20; 1 Tim. 2:5).

◆

Break forth, O beauteous heavenly light,
To herald our salvation;
He stoops to earth—the God of might,
Our hope and expectation.

He comes in human flesh to dwell,
Our God with us, Immanuel,
The night of darkness ending,
Our fallen race befriending.[4]

🌿 Living Insights

"Thanks be to God for His indescribable gift!" the apostle Paul exclaimed (2 Cor. 9:15). And the Incarnation, deity made one with human flesh in Jesus Christ, is just that—indescribable! How can our finite minds begin to grasp such an infinite mercy? Perhaps C. S. Lewis can give us an image to start with.

> Did you ever think, when you were a child, what fun it would be if your toys could come to life? Well suppose you could really have brought them to life. Imagine turning a tin soldier into a real little man. It would involve turning the tin into flesh. And suppose the tin soldier did not like it. He is not interested in flesh; all he sees is that the tin is being spoilt. He thinks you are killing him. He will do everything he can to prevent you. He will not be made into a man if he can help it.
>
> What you would have done about that tin soldier I do not know. But what God did about us was this. The Second Person in God, the Son, became human Himself: was born into the world as an actual man—a real man of a particular height, with hair of a particular colour, speaking a particular language, weighing so many [pounds]. The Eternal Being, who knows everything and who created the whole universe, became not only a man but (before that) a baby, and before that a *foetus* inside a Woman's body. If you want to get the hang of it, think how you would like to become a slug or a crab. . . .
>
> . . . The Man in Christ rose again: not only the God. That is the whole point. For the first time

---

4. Joseph Barlowe, second stanza of "Break Forth, O Beauteous Heavenly Light," © 1986 WORD MUSIC. Used by permission.

we saw a real man. One tin soldier—real tin, just
like the rest—had come fully and splendidly alive.[5]

In the Lerner and Loewe musical *Camelot*, King Arthur is
confronted by Queen Guinevere's infidelity with the king's most
trusted knight, Lancelot. Under the law, she was judged guilty and
sentenced to be burned at the stake. Arthur was caught emotionally
between his love for his wife and his responsibility to the law.
Mordred, Arthur's illegitimate son, articulated the painful position
the king was in:

> Arthur! What a magnificent dilemma! Let her die,
> your life is over; let her live, your life's a fraud.
> Which will it be, Arthur? Do you kill the Queen or
> kill the law?[6]

With tears in his eyes, King Arthur moves to the castle window
to watch the execution. The executioner is waiting for the signal
from the king to light the torch, but Arthur's pain is overpowering.

> I can't! I can't! I can't let her die![7]

To which Mordred replies:

> Well, you're human after all, aren't you, Arthur?
> Human and helpless.[8]

Unlike Arthur, Jesus is not "human and helpless." He is God.
Philippians 2 describes the scene of this King—greater than
Arthur—who left His kingdom behind, who emptied Himself, tak-
ing the form of a man and becoming obedient to the point of death.
A King who left the comforts and splendor of the castle to take
the place of His Guinevere (2 Cor. 8:9). In doing so, both justice
and love were satisfied.

5. C. S. Lewis, *Mere Christianity*, rev. and enl. (1952; reprint, New York, N.Y.: Macmillan
Publishing Co., 1960), pp. 139–40.

6. Alan Jay Lerner, *Camelot*, in the combined volume of *Idylls of the King* and *Camelot*, ed.
Allan Knee (New York, N.Y.: Dell Publishing Co., 1967), p. 241.

7. Lerner, *Camelot*, p. 241.

8. Lerner, *Camelot*, p. 241.

Picture yourself as Guinevere: guilty, awaiting execution. And then the King comes down to put Himself in your place, to pay the penalty for your sin. How will you respond? Can you do anything but fall before Him and wash His feet with your tears?

Chapter 4

JESUS: A LAMB LED TO SLAUGHTER

Isaiah 53:1–7; Selected Scriptures

M ax Lucado, in his excellent book *No Wonder They Call Him the Savior*, writes of the beauty and grandeur of God's dramatic display of love on the cross.

> Nearing the climax of the story, God, motivated by love and directed by divinity, surprised everyone. He became a man. In an untouchable mystery, he disguised himself as a carpenter and lived in a dusty Judean village. Determined to prove his love for his creation, he walked incognito through his own world. His calloused hands touched wounds and his compassionate tongue touched hearts. He became one of us. . . .
>
> But as beautiful as this act of incarnation was, it was not the zenith. Like a master painter God reserved his masterpiece until the end. All the earlier acts of love had been leading to this one. The angels hushed and the heavens paused to witness the finale. God unveils the canvas and the ultimate act of creative compassion is revealed.
>
> God on a cross.
>
> The Creator being sacrificed for the creation. God convincing man once and for all that forgiveness still follows failure.[1]

Death: Jesus' Constant Companion

"Born to die." The phrase has been hung on many a young, hardened criminal. But the cruel shoe fit the sinless Christ better than it did any person in history's hall of shame.

Every day the shadow of the cross stretched long across His

---

1. Max Lucado, *No Wonder They Call Him the Savior* (Portland, Oreg.: Multnomah Press, 1986), pp. 57–58.

path. Before He was even two, an assassination plot by Herod almost put an end to His tender life (Matt. 2:16). By the time He could read, He had learned the Old Testament prophecies of His death (see Ps. 22; Isa. 53). At thirty-three, when most men are beginning their careers, He was ending His.

His Purpose for Coming

Before Mary's pregnancy reached full term, the destiny of her baby was determined. The obituary of Isaiah 53 perched like a vulture over the crib of the Christ child. Sorrow, grief, and pain all synchronized their watches for the time when their day would come, when they would have their chance to bully and beat and bruise Him.

> He was despised and forsaken of men,
> A man of sorrows, and acquainted with grief;
> And like one from whom men hide their face,
> He was despised, and we did not esteem Him.
> Surely our griefs He Himself bore,
> And our sorrows He carried;
> Yet we ourselves esteemed Him stricken,
> Smitten of God, and afflicted.
> But He was pierced through for our transgressions,
> He was crushed for our iniquities;
> The chastening for our well-being fell upon Him,
> And by His scourging we are healed.
> All of us like sheep have gone astray,
> Each of us has turned to his own way;
> But the Lord has caused the iniquity of us all
> To fall on Him.
> He was oppressed and He was afflicted,
> Yet He did not open His mouth;
> Like a lamb that is led to slaughter. (vv. 3–7a)

A lamb led to the slaughter. The tender child would not grow up a doctor . . . or lawyer . . . or rabbi. He would not marry; He would not carry on the family name; He would not even be there to care for His aging mother. He would be a Passover lamb slaughtered as a sacrifice for sin. He would be a baby born to die.

His Comments during Ministry

Not only was the death of Christ prophesied in the Old Testament, it was foretold by His own lips in several New Testament passages.

1. *Matthew 16:21–23.* Following the incident in which Peter acknowledged Jesus to be the Messiah, Jesus began to prepare His disciples for the bitter reality of His imminent suffering and death.

> From that time Jesus Christ began to show His disciples that He must go to Jerusalem, and suffer many things from the elders and chief priests and scribes, and be killed, and be raised up on the third day. And Peter took Him aside and began to rebuke Him, saying, "God forbid it, Lord! This shall never happen to You." But He turned and said to Peter, "Get behind Me, Satan! You are a stumbling block to Me; for you are not setting your mind on God's interests, but man's."

2. *Matthew 17:22–23.* With relentless directness, Jesus continued to chart the road to the cross.

> And while they were gathering together in Galilee, Jesus said to them, "The Son of Man is going to be delivered into the hands of men; and they will kill Him, and He will be raised on the third day." And they were deeply grieved.

3. *Matthew 20:17–19a.* Like a recurring, resonant note in a funeral dirge, Jesus repeated the somber chord concerning His crucifixion.

> And as Jesus was about to go up to Jerusalem, He took the twelve disciples aside by themselves, and on the way He said to them, "Behold, we are going up to Jerusalem; and the Son of Man will be delivered to the chief priests and scribes, and they will condemn Him to death, and will deliver Him to the Gentiles to mock and scourge and crucify Him."

4. *Matthew 26:1–2.* Two days before the storm of the Crucifixion, Jesus was in Jerusalem in the calm eye of the religious city's Passover preparations. Like a captain standing at the mast and scanning the horizon for signs of a storm, Jesus alerted His sailors— His fishers of men—to the waves that were about to batter their ship.

> And it came about that when Jesus had finished all these words, He said to His disciples, "You know that after two days the Passover is coming, and the

Son of Man is to be delivered up for crucifixion."

5. *Matthew 26:6–13.* While Jesus was enjoying an eleventh-hour respite with friends in Bethany, a woman brought "an alabaster vial of very costly perfume" and tenderly poured it out on Him (v. 7). The disciples were indignant at the extravagant waste, explaining that it could have been used to help the poor. But Jesus defended her act of devotion and again revealed His imminent fate.

> But Jesus, aware of this, said to them, "Why do you bother the woman? For she has done a good deed to Me. For the poor you have with you always; but you do not always have Me. For when she poured this perfume upon My body, she did it to prepare Me for burial." (vv. 10–12)

His Statement to the Disciples

It was night when Christ celebrated the Last Supper with His disciples. Several oil lamps dotted the room, sending a gallery of shadows to loiter against the walls, watching. Satan was watching, too, waiting to enter into Judas (John 13:27). Jesus' face was strained; His eyes, intense. A hush fell over the room as He spoke:

> "Truly, truly, I say to you, that one of you will betray Me." (v. 21b)

Their minds spinning, the disciples were soon knocked reeling at Jesus' indicting words to Peter:

> "Truly, truly, I say to you, a cock shall not crow, until you deny Me three times." (v. 38b)

The disciples were stunned. Their leader was about to be betrayed . . . and denied . . . with the betrayal and denial coming from within the ranks of those who had been closest to Him. It was no wonder they were deeply troubled. And it was no surprise— knowing their Savior who had calmed both wind and waves before—that He would now speak to calm their troubled hearts.

> "Let not your heart be troubled; believe in God, believe also in Me. In My Father's house are many dwelling places; if it were not so, I would have told you; for I go to prepare a place for you. And if I go and prepare a place for you, I will come again, and

receive you to Myself; that where I am, there you
may be also." (14:1–3)

Matthew informs us that the Upper Room Discourse was closed
with a hymn; and after the hymn, they went to the Mount of Olives
to pray and await the betrayal (Matt. 26:30).

Arrest and Trials: The Shadow Lengthens

The hymn seemed to hold the shadow of death at bay, but when
it was over, dark and dreadful thoughts lengthened to overtake the
conversation.

> Then Jesus said to them, "You will all fall away
> because of Me this night, for it is written, 'I will
> strike down the shepherd, and the sheep of the flock
> shall be scattered.'" (v. 31)

Pledging his undying loyalty, Peter vowed: "Even though all
may fall away because of You, I will never fall away. . . . Even if
I have to die with You, I will not deny You" (vv. 33, 35). The others
fervently echoed Peter's resolve. But it would be the words of Christ
that would stand. The Shepherd would be struck down; the sheep,
scattered.

In the Garden

Jesus led the disciples to the little garden spot known as Gethsemane to pray (v. 36). He had the others sit and wait while He
took Peter, James, and John with Him. Christ stood on the dark
precipice overlooking the valley of death. For the world to have
light and life, He would have to jump into the blackness to be
dashed upon the altar of jagged rocks below. Fear knotted His
stomach. The agony was unbearable.

> Then He said to them, "My soul is deeply grieved,
> to the point of death; remain here and keep watch
> with Me." And He went a little beyond them, and
> fell on His face and prayed, saying, "My Father, if it
> is possible, let this cup pass from Me; yet not as I
> will, but as Thou wilt." (vv. 38–39)

The vigilante mob arrived (v. 47). The kiss of Judas sealed the
betrayal (vv. 48–49). The Shepherd was taken captive (vv. 50–55).
The sheep were scattered (v. 56).

Before the Authorities

If there was ever a miscarriage of justice, if ever a breach of truth, if ever a blinding of conscience, it happened on this night of infamy when the Creator was brought to trial before His creatures. There were six trials that sleepless night. The first three were conducted by the Jewish authorities and concerned religious questions; the final three concerned civil questions and were conducted by the Roman authorities.[2]

In the first trial, Annas, father-in-law of Caiaphas the high priest, examined Jesus (John 18:12–24). In the second trial, Caiaphas and the Sanhedrin quickly condemned Him, declared—not proved—Him guilty of blasphemy, then mocked and beat Him (Matt. 26:57–68). In the third trial, the Sanhedrin "took counsel against Jesus to put Him to death" (27:1).

Since the Jews could not legally carry out an execution, they turned Christ over to the Roman authorities. Pilate, governor of Judea, presided over this fourth trial (vv. 2, 11–14). The wishy-washy leader found Him innocent (John 18:38b); but when he heard that Jesus had come from Galilee (Luke 23:5–6), he seized the opportunity to pass the judicial buck to Herod, Galilee's governor, who was also in Jerusalem at the time (v. 7). So Herod Antipas presided over the fifth trial (vv. 8–12). But Herod, too, found no guilt in Jesus, and tossed the ball back into Pilate's court (vv. 14b–15).

In the final trial, Pilate again declared Christ innocent (v. 14), but the incensed crowd outside was in a frenzy for blood. Facing a riot, Pilate succumbed to the pressure of the crowd. Washing his hands from the guilt of shedding innocent blood, Pilate gave Jesus over to be crucified (Matt. 27:24–26).

The Cross: *Tetelestai*

A sleepless night of indignity. False witnesses slandering . . . beatings . . . a crown of thorns digging into the King of Kings' head . . . a robe and scepter of mock royalty . . . more scourging . . . more mocking. By 9 A.M. His hands and feet were nailed to a rough-cut cross that was lifted up and dropped with a

---

2. For a more thorough study of the trials Jesus endured, see chapter 11, "A Closer Look at Jesus' Arrest and Trials," in the study guide *A Look at the Book*, coauthored by Lee Hough and Bryce Klabunde, from the Bible-teaching ministry of Charles R. Swindoll (Anaheim, Calif.: Insight for Living, 1994), pp. 101–8.

dull thud into Golgotha's brow. From noon to three, darkness fell over the earth—truly the darkest hours in human history.

John, the disciple whom Christ loved, was an eyewitness to the Crucifixion. He records for us the final minutes of this tragic scene in chapter 19 of his gospel.

> After this, Jesus, knowing that all things had already been accomplished, in order that the Scripture might be fulfilled, said, "I am thirsty." A jar full of sour wine was standing there; so they put a sponge full of the sour wine upon a branch of hyssop, and brought it up to His mouth. When Jesus therefore had received the sour wine, He said, "It is finished!" And He bowed His head, and gave up His spirit. (vv. 28–30)

Jesus took a drink, as if to clear His parched throat so His clarion call could be heard by all: *Tetelestai*—"It is finished!" If the Crucifixion was the darkest moment in history, these words pierced through the clouds like a radiant beam of sunlight.

The words don't refer to the completion of His sufferings but the completion of the task He was born to do—to save His people from their sins (Matt. 1:21). The timber of the cross formed the bridge over sin's troubled waters and spanned hell's chasm, uniting earth and heaven. With the words "It is finished," the bridge was complete. It was a cry of victory, a cry of accomplishment—for with these words, fetters burst, prison walls crumbled, barriers fell, and gates that had been closed for thousands of years began to turn on their rusty hinges.

And yes, it was a cry of relief. Jesus could now exchange His thorns for a crown, His nakedness for a robe, His disgrace for glory, His wounds for worship.

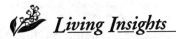 *Living Insights* _____ STUDY ONE

If you're without Christ, you're treading water in a sea of sin. Things may appear calm, and you may feel you've got everything under control now. But one day, you'll go under and sink like a rock and drown. The only life preserver is Jesus; the only way to heaven is the bridge of the cross. You can't swim to the other side on your own strength.

If you're in that situation, you can call out to Jesus—as Peter did when he was sinking—"Lord, save me!" (Matt. 14:30). It doesn't need to be a King James prayer or a Revised Standard confession. It just needs to be from your heart to His. And when these two hearts connect, your bridge to heaven is complete. Isn't it about time you stopped treading and started trusting?

Use the space provided, if you like, to write down your prayer and record the place and date when you crossed over on Christ's bridge. If you have already crossed over, write down your reflections on how that has changed your life—and thank Jesus for spanning the chasm between death and life.

_____

_____

_____

_____

_____

_____

_____

_____

 Living Insights   STUDY TWO

Looking through the shadowy foliage of Gethsemane, we don't see the classic portrait of Christ rendered by the artist. We don't see Him in a snow-white robe kneeling beside a big rock, hands peacefully folded, with a look of serenity in His face as a spotlight from heaven illuminates His golden-brown hair.

Instead, we see a man flat on His face, fists pounding the hard earth in agony. We see a face stained with tears and dirt, hair matted with sweat, facial muscles contorted in pain like the gnarled, twisted olive trees looking on. God was never more human than at this hour.

Are you in the dark garden of Gethsemane? Betrayed by a friend? Deserted by those around you? Abandoned? Lonely? What is your situation?

_____

_____

_____

_____

_____

What feelings are you struggling through?

_____

_____

_____

_____

_____

Christ understands the heart that wants the cup of suffering to pass from it. He knows the inner torment of trying to balance our honest rage at the unfairness of life with reverence and obedience to a sovereign, holy God.

He knows.

He has writhed in your agony Himself.

So, in your prayers, pray with Him beside you. In your wrenching pain, feel His tears that know your rawness. In time, He will help you to the point where you can say, "Yet not as I will, but as Thou wilt."

In time.

His is one hand that will not rush you.

Chapter 5

JESUS: TRIUMPHANT OVER THE GRAVE

John 19:30–20:29

It was a morning like any other in the ancient Roman city. Children romped just as they did yesterday and the day before that. Men and women went about their business as usual: working hard in the bright sunlight and resting easy in the cool shade of the mountain; worshiping their idols in the pagan temples; eating, drinking, and living life in their normal, everyday way. Yet in a few precious hours, they would all be dead—the fury of Mount Vesuvius would erupt to encase Pompeii in a tomb of lava for centuries to come.

About forty years before Pompeii was destroyed, another eruption had taken place that shook the foundations of heaven and earth. An ordinary woman had come to the tomb of her beloved friend, just as she had probably done the day before and the day before that. But today, she was horrified by an open grave—the body missing, the stone rolled away. She ran away in her terror and grief, but what she didn't know then was that the tomb had erupted with the power of God. The crucified Son of God had risen, triumphantly conquering death and bringing new life to a human race encased in sin since time began.

Jesus' Prediction of His Resurrection

Paul reasons in 1 Corinthians 15 that "if Christ has not been raised, your faith is worthless" (v. 17a) and "if the dead are not raised, let us eat and drink, for tomorrow we die" (v. 32b). If Jesus did not rise from the dead, Christianity is no better than the pagan religions of Pompeii. But His triumph over the grave gave Christianity a unique distinctive: its founder *lives!* Early in the Gospel accounts, Jesus predicted not only His death—but also His resurrection.

A Sign Requested

In 1 Corinthians 1:22, Paul writes that the "Jews ask for signs, and Greeks search for wisdom." This tendency on the part of the Jews to walk by sight as opposed to faith is illustrated in Matthew 12, where the scribes and Pharisees demanded a sign from Jesus.

But He refused to pander to these religious voyeurs and answered with a barbed rebuke:

> "An evil and adulterous generation craves for a sign; and yet no sign shall be given to it but the sign of Jonah the prophet." (v. 39)

"The Sign of Jonah"

Instead of an immediate, nickel-and-dime show of power, Jesus announced a future sign so spectacular that one would have to be blind to miss it.

> "For just as Jonah was three days and three nights in the belly of the sea monster, so shall the Son of Man be three days and three nights in the heart of the earth." (v. 40)

Quoting Jonah 1:17, Jesus predicted His resurrection and claimed that His interment would last no longer than three days and nights. Just as Jonah emerged alive from the belly of the great fish, so Jesus would be released from the bowels of the earth.[1]

Pertinent Issues Related to Jesus' Resurrection

If we build a bridge from Matthew 12 to John 19, we move directly from "the sign of Jonah" to the sight of Jesus on Golgotha. In Matthew 12, we see Him bristling with life as He clashes with the Pharisees. In John 19, we see Him lay down His sword at the cross in a final act of submission.

Certainty of His Death

Some have sought to explain away Christ's appearances after His death with something known as the "swoon theory." This theory says Christ did not die but merely fainted from the physical and emotional trauma of the cross and later revived in the coolness of the tomb. The evidence, however, conclusively argues against this speculation. First, the testimony of Scripture clearly states that Jesus died.

When Jesus therefore had received the sour wine,

---

1. Other passages where Jesus spoke of His resurrection are Matthew 16:21; 17:22–23; 20:18–19; Mark 10:32–34.

He said, "It is finished!" And He bowed His head, and gave up His spirit. (John 19:30)

Second, the actions of the soldiers around the cross corroborate the claims.

The soldiers therefore came, and broke the legs of the first man, and of the other man who was crucified with Him; but coming to Jesus, when they saw that He was already dead, they did not break His legs. (vv. 32–33)[2]

Third, the testimony of the physiological data supports the fact of Christ's death.

But one of the soldiers pierced His side with a spear, and immediately there came out blood and water.[3] (v. 34)

Finally, the actions of the burial party indicate the certainty of Jesus' death (vv. 38–42). Had there been any indication of life, those preparing Him for burial would have tried to revive Him. Instead, they embalmed the body and placed it in the tomb.[4]

Material Evidence

In John 20:1–7, three important pieces of material evidence support Christ's resurrection: the displaced stone, the empty tomb, and the linen wrappings.

Now on the first day of the week Mary Magdalene came early to the tomb, while it was still dark, and saw the stone already taken away from the tomb. And so she ran and came to Simon Peter, and to

---

2. The normal cause of death in crucifixion was suffocation. The chest cavity would collapse under the hanging weight of the body. In order to breathe, the victim would have to push up with the legs to a more erect position. To hurry death, the legs would be broken, thus preventing the victim from being able to breathe.

3. When the blood's thicker plasma separates from the thinner serum, it is a sign of certain death.

4. According to the burial customs of that time, a corpse was wrapped tightly with cloth in which aromatic spices were interspersed. This covered the stench of death and formed an adhesive seal around the body. We are told that one hundred pounds of aloes and myrrh were purchased for Christ's burial. The tightly wrapped cloths with the gummy spices formed a mummylike cocoon, as described in the account where Jesus raised Lazarus (John 11:44).

the other disciple whom Jesus loved, and said to them, "They have taken away the Lord out of the tomb, and we do not know where they have laid Him." Peter therefore went forth, and the other disciple, and they were going to the tomb. And the two were running together; and the other disciple ran ahead faster than Peter, and came to the tomb first; and stooping and looking in, he saw the linen wrappings lying there; but he did not go in. Simon Peter therefore also came, following him, and entered the tomb; and he beheld the linen wrappings lying there, and the face-cloth, which had been on His head, not lying with the linen wrappings, but rolled up in a place by itself.

The burial wrappings, made rigid by the resin from the spices, formed a shell that now lay empty on the cold rock slab in the tomb. Only the face covering, which was a band wound like a turban, was disheveled and rolled up in a place off to one side. The immediate impression of Mary Magdalene was that the body had been stolen (v. 2). Apparently, this was also the initial reaction of Peter and John (vv. 8–9).

But logically, who would have kidnapped it? Neither the Jews nor the Romans wanted an empty tomb. They wanted Christ dead and buried. If they had stolen it, they would merely have had to produce the body, and the claim of the Resurrection would have been discredited. The guards, whose very lives were at stake in safeguarding the body, wouldn't have dared to steal it or allow it to be stolen. Finally, the alarm expressed by the disciples precludes them from being suspects. Neither friend nor foe had a logical motive to kidnap the body. Again, the evidence points to a literal, bodily resurrection.

Physical Appearances

The New Testament records no fewer than eleven physical encounters with the risen Christ. These encounters occurred at different times, in different places, and with a variety of individuals. It has often been argued that these people merely had grief-induced hallucinations. However, Jesus once appeared to more than five hundred people at one time (1 Cor. 15:6). For so many people to have shared the same hallucination at the same time strains the imagination far more than the probability of Christ's bodily resurrection.

John, an eyewitness to the death of Christ, records four postresurrection appearances: one with Mary outside the tomb (John 20:11–18), one with the disciples behind closed doors (vv. 19–23), one with Thomas (vv. 24–29), and one with the disciples on the beach by the Sea of Tiberias (21:1–23). Christ's appearance to Thomas, though, is particularly awesome and arresting.

> But Thomas, one of the twelve, called Didymus, was not with them when Jesus came. The other disciples therefore were saying to him, "We have seen the Lord!" But he said to them, "Unless I shall see in His hands the imprint of the nails, and put my finger into the place of the nails, and put my hand into His side, I will not believe."
>
> And after eight days again His disciples were inside, and Thomas with them. Jesus came, the doors having been shut, and stood in their midst, and said, "Peace be with you." Then He said to Thomas, "Reach here your finger, and see My hands; and reach here your hand, and put it into My side; and be not unbelieving, but believing." Thomas answered and said to Him, "My Lord and my God!" Jesus said to him, "Because you have seen Me, have you believed? Blessed are they who did not see, and yet believed." (20:24–29)

Historical Results

At the time of the Cross, the disciples had scattered like scared sheep (Matt. 26:56). After seeing the empty tomb, they believed with Mary that someone had stolen the body, and they went away to their own homes (John 20:2, 8–10). There they hid, cowering, shuttered away in fear of the Jews (v. 19).

However, after they had seen the risen Christ, this weak-kneed band of deserters turned the world upside down (see Acts 17:6). Even Peter, who denied Christ so emphatically, preached boldly about Him in the very city where He was only recently executed (Acts 2:14–36). The descent of the Holy Spirit and the birth of the Church are two other historical ramifications of the Resurrection (Acts 1–2).

The Lasting Benefits

Never were the arms of God opened so wide as when they were outstretched on the cross. Like a father embracing his prodigal son, the arms of Jesus reached out to give the embrace of forgiveness to all who would come home. May God give you the grace to look at the nail prints in the hands of the risen Savior and fall on your face before Him, as did Thomas, proclaiming through tears: "My Lord and my God!" For the Resurrection assures us not only that Jesus is God, but that we are forgiven and will also be resurrected after our death to live forever in His presence (1 Cor. 15).

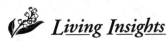 *Living Insights* STUDY ONE

In our unstretched, rigid imaginations, we strain to make room in our thinking for miracles. Like Thomas, we are so used to living by sight rather than by faith that we are constantly looking for hands with nail prints. We are used to working with statistical probabilities and empirical evidence, while God characteristically works with impossibilities and the evidence of things not seen (Luke 1:37; Heb. 11:1).

How supple is your imagination? When is the last time the impossible rearranged the furniture of your thinking? Or sight bowed to faith in your relationship with Christ?

If you're stumped for an answer to these questions, maybe you've got God too small and limited in your thinking. As an encouragement to stretch your realm of possibilities, remember Jesus' words to Thomas: "Blessed are they who did not see, and yet believed" (John 20:29).

 Living Insights STUDY TWO

Now on the first day of the week Mary Magdalene came early to the tomb, while it was still dark, and saw the stone already taken away from the tomb. And so she ran and came to Simon Peter, and to the other disciple whom Jesus loved, and said to them, "They have taken away the Lord out of the tomb, and we do not know where they have laid Him." . . .

But Mary was standing outside the tomb weeping.
(John 20:1–2, 11)

Like Mary, do you have anything you're grieving over? Maybe it's the death of a relationship. Maybe it's the death of a dream. Maybe it's the death of your desires. Whatever it is, it is entirely possible for God to bring new life out of that situation—no matter how dark the tomb or how heavy the stone that seals it.

Regarding His own death, Jesus said: "Truly, truly, I say to you, unless a grain of wheat falls into the earth and dies, it remains by itself alone; but if it dies, it bears much fruit" (John 12:24).

Are you grieving over a dead grain? What is it?

_____

_____

What blade of hope can you see sprouting to the surface from that dead grain?

_____

_____

_____

What fruit can you envision coming from that sprout in the months and years ahead?

_____

_____

_____

In what ways can that fruit nourish you or those around you?[5]

_____

_____

_____

5. This Living Insight has been adapted from the study guide *Issues and Answers in Jesus' Day*, coauthored by Ken Gire, from the Bible-teaching ministry of Charles R. Swindoll (Fullerton, Calif.: Insight for Living, 1990), pp. 26–27.

Chapter 6

JESUS: ASCENDED AND SEATED IN HEAVEN

Acts 1:6–11; Ephesians 1:18–23

There are times when it would be great to telephone God—collect! Or to pull God aside to ask a few questions. Or, at least, to write Him a letter. In the book *Children's Letters to God*, the authors have compiled an amusing yet insightful scrapbook of thoughts and questions children have posed to God. Here are a few samples.

> Dear God,
>> Count me in
>>> Your friend
>>> Herbie

> Dear God,
>> I wrote you before do you remember? Well I did what I promised. But you did not send me the horse yet. What about it?
>>> Lewis

> Dear God,
>> Do you get your angels to do all the work? Mommy says we are her angels and we have to do everything.
>>> Love,
>>> Maria

> Dear God,
>> When you started the earth and put people there and all the animals and grass and the stars did you get verey tired? I have a lot of other questions too.
>>> Very truly yours
>>> Sherman[1]

---

1. *Children's Letters to God*, comp. Eric Marshall and Stuart Hample (New York, N.Y.: Simon and Schuster, Pocket Books, 1966).

Questions. Regardless of how foolish or childish they may seem, they're the best way to get specific answers. A few questions this study may have prompted are: Now that Jesus has died and risen from the grave, what is He doing? Since Jesus was bodily raised from the dead, does He still operate within a body, or is He just a spirit? When He ascended from earth to heaven, did His position change from what it was originally?

With these questions, we'll raise our hands to find out about the present ministry of Jesus—since His ascension. And remember, the only foolish question is the unasked one.

The Ascension: When Jesus Christ Left Earth

In Acts 1:1–11, we are told that for forty days after His resurrection Jesus remained in contact with His followers. He spoke, ate, slept, encouraged, instructed, and essentially did all that He had done during His three and a half years with them (see Luke 24). But then it was time for Him to depart. Moments before He ascended to heaven, the disciples raised their hands to wave an eager question before their teacher.

> And so when they had come together, they were asking Him, saying, "Lord, is it at this time You are restoring the kingdom to Israel?" (Acts 1:6)

Patiently but firmly, Jesus told them what they didn't need to worry about and, in doing so, redirected their attention to the page of God's plan that was soon to be turned.

> He said to them, "It is not for you to know times or epochs which the Father has fixed by His own authority; but you shall receive power when the Holy Spirit has come upon you; and you shall be My witnesses both in Jerusalem, and in all Judea and Samaria, and even to the remotest part of the earth." (vv. 7–8)

With the promise of the Holy Spirit's presence and power, Jesus spoke His last words on earth and ascended into heaven.

> And after He had said these things, He was lifted up while they were looking on, and a cloud received Him out of their sight. (v. 9)

46

As He rose into the clouds and disappeared, the awestruck disciples craned their necks and squinted for one last look.

Historical Fact

Three facets of the Ascension assure us that it was a historical fact. First, it was *public*—"He was lifted up *while they were looking on*" (v. 9, emphasis added). Second, it didn't happen so quickly that no one could be sure of what they saw; but it was *gradual*—"while He was blessing them, He parted from them" (Luke 24:51). And third, it was *literal*—in His bodily form Jesus was "lifted up . . . and a cloud received Him out of their sight" (Acts 1:9).

Practical Value

At first glance the doctrine of the Ascension seems like the clouds into which Christ ascended—distant and nebulous. However, understanding the Ascension helps us in at least four ways.

First, it helps us appreciate the credibility of Christ. He said He would have to leave the disciples one day (John 13:33, 36; 14:1–6), and since they actually saw Him leave, the credibility of Christ's word is underscored once more in our thinking.

Second, if Christ had not ascended, the Spirit would not have been given to us.

> "But I tell you the truth, it is to your advantage that
> I go away; for if I do not go away, the Helper shall
> not come to you; but if I go, I will send Him to you."
> (16:7)

Third, without His ascension, we would never have received our spiritual gifts.

> But to each one of us grace was given according to
> the measure of Christ's gift. Therefore it says,
> "When He ascended on high,
> He led captive a host of captives,
> And He gave gifts to men." (Eph. 4:7–8)

Fourth, in Jesus' literal, bodily ascension we have a historic reminder that His return will also be a literal, bodily return.

> "This Jesus, who has been taken up from you into
> heaven, will come in just the same way as you have
> watched Him go into heaven." (Acts 1:11)

Entrance: When Jesus Christ Returned to Heaven

Moving from Acts 1 to Ephesians 1, we leave earth and glimpse the heavenly side of the Ascension, where the Father raised Christ from the dead,

> and seated Him at His right hand in the heavenly places, far above all rule and authority and power and dominion, and every name that is named, not only in this age, but also in the one to come. And He put all things in subjection under His feet, and gave Him as head over all things to the church, which is His body, the fulness of Him who fills all in all. (Eph. 1:20b–23)

In direct contrast to the crown of thorns, scepter, and robe the world gave to Jesus in mockery, the Father's act of receiving His Son into heaven was His expression of final approval for Christ's redemptive mission. The Father, in a royal coronation ceremony, placed the King of Kings on His rightful throne "far above all rule and authority and power and dominion." And in putting "all things in subjection under His feet," the Father gave Jesus dominion not only over His enemies (see Ps. 2; 110) but over the Church as well (Col. 1:17–20).

Seated: When Jesus Was Enthroned

Although Christ's earthly mission of redemption is complete— "having offered one sacrifice for sins for all time" (Heb. 10:12)— His heavenly ministry and involvement with us is continuing. The writer to the Hebrews informs us that Jesus is presently our high priest and mediator, our Lord and master, and our companion and friend.

Our High Priest and Mediator

We have a great high priest—Jesus, the God-Man—who, though sinless, is sympathetic.

> Since then we have a great high priest who has passed through the heavens, Jesus the Son of God, let us hold fast our confession. For we do not have a high priest who cannot sympathize with our weaknesses, but one who has been tempted in all things

48

as we are, yet without sin. Let us therefore draw near
with confidence to the throne of grace, that we may
receive mercy and may find grace to help in time of
need. (4:14–16)

Also, because Jesus' priesthood is permanent, He will eternally
defend us before God from Satan's accusations and constantly inter-
cede to forgive our sin and guilt (see Rom. 8:33–34; 1 John 2:1).

Our Sovereign Lord and Master

Jesus ministers not only as our great high priest but as our
sovereign Lord and master as well.

But of the Son He says, . . .
"Thou hast made him for a little while lower
than the angels;
Thou hast crowned him with glory and honor,
And hast appointed him over the works of Thy
hands;
Thou hast put all things in subjection under
his feet." (Heb. 1:8a; 2:7–8)

Jesus is intimately involved with mankind by sovereignly calling
out a people for Himself, sovereignly functioning as the head of the
Church, and sovereignly directing the affairs of life.

Our Constant Companion and Friend

Because Jesus was God in the flesh and related to people in
eyeball-to-eyeball friendships (see John 11:1–44), we are assured
that the distance of His heavenly throne won't separate us from
His presence. Repeatedly, the writer to the Hebrews exalts the deity
and majesty of the enthroned Savior. Yet he is careful to underscore
that this great high priest, this almighty and sovereign Lord, is also
a close companion and friend. Christ is not ashamed to count us
as His most intimate relations.

For both He who sanctifies and those who are sanc-
tified are all from one Father; for which reason He
is not ashamed to call them brethren. (Heb. 2:11)

And like a good friend, He encourages us.

In the same way God, desiring even more to show
to the heirs of the promise the unchangeableness of

49

His purpose, interposed with an oath, in order that by two unchangeable things, in which it is impossible for God to lie, we may have strong encouragement, we who have fled for refuge in laying hold of the hope set before us. (6:17–18)

A friend isn't capricious in the relationship, isn't on-again, off-again, isn't fickle. A friend is someone you can count on. And what a friend we have in Jesus—"the same yesterday and today, yes and forever" (Heb. 13:8).

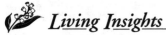 *Living Insights* STUDY ONE

The kingdom of God is a future era on earth when Jesus will return to rule His creation. In the meantime, Jesus rules from heaven. His preceptive will in heaven is done on earth to the extent that we have enthroned Him in our lives as King (Matt. 6:9–13). You may have received Jesus years ago as Savior, but have you enthroned Him as Lord? Are all things in your life put in subjection to Him?

In what areas of your life do you resist recognizing that He is sovereign? Business? Sexuality? Finances? School? Write down the areas of your life that still have your will and needs on the throne.

_____

_____

_____

Why isn't Christ first in these areas? Are you afraid of what might happen if you are not in control? Does the pleasure of your lifestyle seem more real to you than the need to obey Jesus' commands? Try to define what is keeping you from putting all your things in subjection to Him.

_____

_____

_____

_____

_____

Don't mock Him in a false display by putting a robe on His shoulders and a scepter in His hands, pretending, as the Roman soldiers did, to honor Him. Maybe an ascension needs to take place in your life. Enthrone Him, won't you? For He is not only the rightful King, but the *worthy* King. Worthy to be exalted, honored, obeyed, and most of all—worthy to be loved.

> And I looked, and I heard the voice of many angels around the throne and the living creatures and the elders; and the number of them was myriads of myriads, and thousands of thousands, saying with a loud voice,
>> "Worthy is the Lamb that was slain to receive power and riches and wisdom and might and honor and glory and blessing."
> And every created thing which is in heaven and on the earth and under the earth and on the sea, and all things in them, I heard saying,
>> "To Him who sits on the throne, and to the Lamb, be blessing and honor and glory and dominion forever and ever."
> And the four living creatures kept saying, "Amen." And the elders fell down and worshiped. (Rev. 5:11–14)

 Living Insights

What a beautiful testimony to the humility of Christ that He is not ashamed of us. Think of it! The God of all creation, the great high priest, the sovereign King—not ashamed to have us in His family, not ashamed to call us brothers. Us! When you think about it, it's staggering. But what is even more staggering, more unbelievable, is that we might somehow, in some way, or in some set of circumstances be ashamed of Him.

> Jesus! and shall it ever be,
> A mortal man ashamed of Thee?
> Ashamed of Thee, whom angels praise,
> Whose glories shine through endless days?
>
> Ashamed of Jesus? Sooner far
> Let evening blush to own a star.

He sheds the beams of light divine
O'er this benighted soul of mine.

Ashamed of Jesus? Just as soon
Let midnight be ashamed of noon.
'Tis midnight with my soul till He,
Bright Morning Star, bids darkness flee.

Ashamed of Jesus, that dear Friend
On whom my hopes of heav'n depend?
No; when I blush, be this my shame,
That I no more revere His name.

Ashamed of Jesus? Yes, I may
When I've no guilt to wash away,
No tear to wipe, no good to crave,
No fear to quell, no soul to save.

Till then—nor is my boasting vain—
Till then I boast a Savior slain;
And oh, may this my glory be,
That Christ is not ashamed of me![2]

2. Joseph Grigg and Benjamin Francis, "Jesus! and Shall It Ever Be," in *The Lutheran Hymnal* (Saint Louis, Mo.: Concordia Publishing House, 1941), no. 346.

Chapter 7

JESUS: HIS PROMISED RETURN

Selected Scriptures

It was the war-torn Pacific, March 11, 1942. Sixty-two-year-old General Douglas MacArthur, under orders from President Roosevelt, secretly slipped away from the Japanese-held Philippines and, in a minor miracle, made his way to Australia.

Before General MacArthur left, however, he resolutely promised, "I shall return."[1] More than two and a half years later, on October 20, 1944, he stood again on the soil of the Philippines and announced triumphantly, "I have returned. By the grace of Almighty God, our forces stand again on Philippine soil."[2]

If a man can have that type of resolve and credibility, how much more the Son of God?

Of course, the real question is not whether Jesus will return, or even when, but whether we will be ready to face Him when He does. Doctrinally, most of us believe Jesus will return. Emotionally, however, most have never been affected by this doctrine.

Scripture tells us that the whole of creation eagerly awaits and anxiously longs for the Savior's return—standing on tiptoes, squinting its eyes, heart aching for the time He will come to renew and restore the cosmos.

Can that be said of you? Is the return of Christ simply a tenet of the faith you give an assenting nod to? Or do you *eagerly await* His return—as the Filipinos did MacArthur or as the New Testament church did Jesus (see 1 Cor. 1:7; Phil. 3:20)?

Christ's Own Predictions of His Return

One possible reason for the lack of emotional commitment to Christ's return is that many of us are not intellectually convinced of it. The Scriptures, however, are abrim with enough references to convince the most skeptical of Thomases.

---

1. General Douglas MacArthur, as quoted in *Bartlett's Familiar Quotations*, 15th ed., rev. and enl., ed. Emily Morison Beck (Boston, Mass.: Little, Brown and Co., 1980), p. 771.

2. MacArthur, *Bartlett's*, p. 771.

Several Scriptures

As the disciples watched Jesus ascend, two angels stood beside them and said:

> "Men of Galilee, why do you stand looking into the sky? This Jesus, who has been taken up from you into heaven, will come in just the same way as you have watched Him go into heaven."[3] (Acts 1:11)

Back in Mark 13, Jesus Himself climactically unfolded His grand entrance, describing the terrible drama of the Tribulation and the heroic rescue of His imperiled children.

> "But in those days, after that tribulation, the sun will be darkened, and the moon will not give its light, and the stars will be falling from heaven, and the powers that are in the heavens will be shaken. And then they will see the Son of Man coming in clouds with great power and glory. And then He will send forth the angels, and will gather together His elect from the four winds, from the farthest end of the earth, to the farthest end of heaven." (vv. 24–27)

Jesus' words, reaffirmed by the two heavenly messengers in Acts 1, resolutely proclaim, "I *will* return."

General Characteristics

Jesus informs us in Mark 13:31–32 that although His coming is certain, no one—not the angels, not even He Himself—knows the time of His return; only the Father knows. However, Jesus has provided certain unmistakable indicators to announce the imminency of His return. Just as emerging buds on winter's brittle branches harbinger spring, so certain signals will herald the return of Christ (vv. 28–29). In Matthew 24, Jesus explained the nature of these burgeoning signs.

> And as He was sitting on the Mount of Olives, the disciples came to Him privately, saying, "Tell us, when will these things be, and what will be the sign of Your coming, and of the end of the age?" And

---

3. The promise in Acts 1 is not a new revelation but merely an echo of Christ's earlier words to His disciples in John 14:1–3.

Jesus answered and said to them, "See to it that no one misleads you. For many will come in My name, saying, 'I am the Christ,' and will mislead many." (vv. 3–5)

With private candor, Jesus warned that religious deception will mark the beginning of the end times. Other nubs on the branch will be political unrest along with agricultural and geophysical upheaval.

"And you will be hearing of wars and rumors of wars; see that you are not frightened, for those things must take place, but that is not yet the end. For nation will rise against nation, and kingdom against kingdom, and in various places there will be famines and earthquakes. But all these things are merely the beginning of birth pangs." (vv. 6–8)

Certainly, these signs have existed since the dawn of time, but it is the frequency and intensity of the signs that will toll the twilight knell on earthly history. To alert us to the start of this final age, Christ uses the metaphor of childbirth. Like "the beginning of birth pangs," wars will become more frequent, more intense. The earth will be a woman in labor, writhing in pain and agony. Turning to a physician's account of this process, we find that Luke charts the patient's progress with even more meticulous detail.

"And there will be great earthquakes, and in various places plagues and famines; and there will be terrors and great signs from heaven." (Luke 21:11)

Plagues and cosmic chaos . . . but before that the worldwide cry of persecuted saints.

"But before all these things, they will lay their hands on you and will persecute you, delivering you to the synagogues and prisons, bringing you before kings and governors for My name's sake. It will lead to an opportunity for your testimony. So make up your minds not to prepare beforehand to defend yourselves; for I will give you utterance and wisdom which none of your opponents will be able to resist or refute. But you will be delivered up even by parents and brothers and relatives and friends, and they will put some of you to death." (vv. 12–16)

The Distinction between the Rapture and the Second Advent

Regardless of how black the clouds will get on the horizon of the end times, the silver lining on their edges is formed by the radiant Son who shines behind them. For Jesus has arranged an airlift—an emergency evacuation—to deliver His children from the terrors of this Tribulation[4] (see 1 Thess. 4:17).

"Operation Airlift"—Saints Removed

Of all the mysterious scenes to occur in the sky, none will be so startling and strange as the Rapture of the Church. Paul hints at this mystery in 1 Corinthians 15:51–53.

> Behold, I tell you a mystery; we shall not all sleep, but we shall all be changed, in a moment, in the twinkling of an eye, at the last trumpet; for the trumpet will sound, and the dead will be raised imperishable, and we shall be changed. For this perishable must put on the imperishable, and this mortal must put on immortality.

In 1 Thessalonians 4:13–18, the veil to this mystery is further lifted.

> But we do not want you to be uninformed, brethren, about those who are asleep, that you may not grieve, as do the rest who have no hope. For if we believe that Jesus died and rose again, even so God will bring with Him those who have fallen asleep in Jesus. For this we say to you by the word of the Lord, that we who are alive, and remain until the coming of the Lord, shall not precede those who have fallen asleep. For the Lord Himself will descend from heaven with a shout, with the voice of the archangel, and with the trumpet of God; and the dead in Christ shall rise first. Then we who are alive and remain shall be caught up together with them in the clouds to meet the Lord in the air, and thus we shall

---

4. For more detailed information on the Tribulation, see Revelation 6–19. For an in-depth study, consult *Things to Come* by J. Dwight Pentecost (Findlay, Ohio: Dunham Publishing Co., 1958), pp. 229–369.

always be with the Lord. Therefore comfort one another with these words.

The Judgment Seat of Christ—Saints Rewarded

After we are taken into Christ's arms, we will be ushered before His throne and rewarded for the life we have lived on earth. Here, the true scales of justice will weigh the substance of our deeds, and Jesus Himself will assay the purity of our hearts.

> For we must all appear before the judgment seat of Christ, that each one may be recompensed for his deeds in the body, according to what he has done, whether good or bad. (2 Cor. 5:10; see also Rom. 14:10–12; 1 Cor. 3:10–15)

Jesus' Return to Earth—Saints Reigning

At the climax of the war of wars, Armageddon, the King of Kings will return to earth to establish His rightful throne. With Him will be all the rewarded believers, who will assume roles of responsibility and rule with Him in His kingdom. This millennial reign of Christ will be a golden age of peace and prosperity on the earth (Rev. 19–20), ushered in by His Second Advent.

In the Meantime . . . What about Today?

Peter poses a penetrating question as we consider the end times and the promise of Jesus' return:

> Since all these things are to be destroyed in this way, what sort of people ought you to be? (2 Pet. 3:11a)

Are we to be prophecy freaks, fanatically walking the streets with placards reading The End Is Near? Are we to sell all our material belongings and wait on a hillside for the Lord's coming? Or should we play the epicurean tune and "eat, drink, and be merry," divorcing ourselves from world events out of our control? No, Peter urges none of these extremes. Rather, his counsel is sane and sensible.

> But according to His promise we are looking for new heavens and a new earth, in which righteousness dwells.
> Therefore, beloved, since you look for these things, be diligent to be found by Him in peace, spotless and

57

blameless. . . . Be on your guard lest, being carried away by the error of unprincipled men, you fall from your own steadfastness, but grow in the grace and knowledge of our Lord and Savior Jesus Christ. To Him be the glory, both now and to the day of eternity. Amen. (3:13–14, 17b–18)

Not panicked lives, but peaceful. Not polluted lifestyles, but pure. Ever growing in the grace and knowledge of our returning Savior, Jesus Christ.

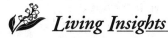 *Living Insights*

All over our world today, wars and rumors of wars abound, and natural disasters rock the earth. From Africa to AIDS, brushfires of famine and plague rage out of control. Meanwhile, the population bomb continues to tick, hands upright, pointing to the eleventh hour of planet Earth. But in the midst of that anxious and dramatic hour, Jesus offers us the relief of His return.

> "Let not your heart be troubled; believe in God, believe also in Me. In My Father's house are many dwelling places; if it were not so, I would have told you; for I go to prepare a place for you. And if I go and prepare a place for you, I will come again, and receive you to Myself; that where I am, there you may be also." (John 14:1–3)

Can you honestly say you have the assurance that when Jesus returns He will receive you? Not hope, not wish, but *assurance?*

If you have personally accepted Christ as your Savior, you can be confident that He has prepared a place for *you.* Sometimes, though, you doubt that, don't you? Be honest now—sometimes we all feel unworthy of Christ's great promise, especially when we've really goofed or have committed that same sin once again.

Not surprisingly, God knows this about us too, and He has graciously given us the following words of comfort so that we *can* be assured. Take some time to read through these verses of His, prayerfully; then write down the assurance they give you. And let not *your* heart be troubled anymore!

John 1:12 _____

John 5:24 _____

_____

John 6:37 _____

_____

John 10:27–29 _____

_____

Romans 8:15–16 _____

_____

Romans 8:35–39 _____

_____

Hebrews 7:24–25 _____

_____

 Living Insights _____ STUDY TWO

Jesus' prophetic message not only comforts us about our future, it also asks for a response in our daily lives. In 2 Peter 3, the apostle pinpoints that response as *growing in the grace and knowledge of Jesus, our Lord.*

In the study guide *Conquering through Conflict*, Lee Hough challenges us to examine this mandate for growth.[5]

> Remember how exciting it was to lean against the kitchen wall and have Mom or Dad measure how tall you were? As children, we yearned to grow up and have somebody mark our progress along the

5. This Living Insight is from the study guide *Conquering through Conflict: A Study of 2 Peter,* coauthored by Lee Hough, from the Bible-teaching ministry of Charles R. Swindoll (Fullerton, Calif.: Insight for Living, 1990), pp. 83–84.

way. But when we finally reached that zenith called adulthood, many of us made the mistake of thinking that all our growing years were over.

. . . Peter counters this mistaken belief with his earnest entreaty to *"grow* in the grace and knowledge of our Lord and Savior Jesus Christ" (2 Pet. 3:18, emphasis added). What kind of progress are you making in this area? Why not use the following questions to mark the rate of your spiritual growth.

Is your life reflecting the grace of Christ? In what specific ways?

In what ways do you know the Lord better this year than last?

How has the grace and knowledge of Christ impacted your life practically?

What are some areas you feel the need to grow in?

Take these areas before God right now. Don't put it off, for as J. I. Packer reminds us,

The New Testament makes plain that this

life, in which bodies grow and wear out while characters get fixed, is an antechamber, dressing-room and moral gymnasium where, whether we know it or not, we all in fact prepare ourselves for a future life which will correspond for each of us to what we have chosen to be, and will have in it more of joy for some and distress for others than this world ever knows.[6]

6. J. I. Packer, *God Has Spoken* (1979; reprint, Grand Rapids, Mich.: Baker Book House, 1988), p. 10.

Chapter 8

JESUS: HE IS LORD

Ephesians 3:14–4:32

Paul's prayer for the Ephesians—and, ultimately, all believers—
was "that Christ may dwell in your hearts" (Eph. 3:17a; compare John 14:23). When we receive Jesus as *Savior*, we open the
doors of our hearts and let Him enter to dine and reside and fellowship with us (see Rev. 3:20).

However, committing to Him as *Lord* is like transferring the
title of our hearts to Him. He comes not only to dine but also to
redesign our lives; not only to reside but also to renovate.

He goes through every room—not simply to spring-clean our
hearts with Windexed works and Pine Soled platitudes but to completely remodel them from ceiling to cellar. With the meticulous
precision of an architect, He takes out a door here, puts in a window
there; He erects a wall where there was permissiveness, takes out a
dark closet where pet sins were once privately fed and nurtured.
He rewires our thinking, replumbs our emotions, and expands the
square footage of our hearts to dimensions we never dreamed were
possible (see Eph. 3:20).

What was once a hovel, Jesus transforms into a home—an
Architectural Digest delight!

Jesus: Lord of All My Externals

As Lord, His decisions are comprehensive, touching what goes
on inside as well as what happens on the outside. He is Lord of our
relationships, our work, our circumstances, and our bodies—where
the rubber of faith meets the road of real life.

Lord of My Relationships

Paul's prayer in Ephesians 4 reveals a lot about relationships.

> I, therefore, the prisoner of the Lord, entreat you
> to walk in a manner worthy of the calling with
> which you have been called, with all humility and
> gentleness, with patience, showing forbearance to
> one another in love, being diligent to preserve the
> unity of the Spirit in the bond of peace. (vv. 1–3)

Is Jesus Lord of your relationships? Does *humility* regulate them? Look at the example of Christ and see if your attitude parallels His.

> Do nothing from selfishness or empty conceit, but with humility of mind let each of you regard one another as more important than himself; do not merely look out for your own personal interests, but also for the interests of others. Have this attitude in yourselves which was also in Christ Jesus, who, although He existed in the form of God, did not regard equality with God a thing to be grasped, but emptied Himself, taking the form of a bond-servant, and being made in the likeness of men. (Phil. 2:3–7)

After humility, the next quality on Paul's list is *gentleness* (Eph. 4:2). Are you gentle with others? How do you respond to your children? To your employer or employees? To your neighbor? We have only to put our ear to the door of Mary and Martha's home to hear the gentle words of Christ calm a potentially volatile situation (compare Prov. 15:1).

> But Martha was distracted with all her preparations; and she came up to Him, and said, "Lord, do You not care that my sister has left me to do all the serving alone? Then tell her to help me." But the Lord answered and said to her, "Martha, Martha, you are worried and bothered about so many things; but only a few things are necessary, really only one, for Mary has chosen the good part, which shall not be taken away from her." (Luke 10:40–42)

Patience, forbearance, love, diligence, unity, peace . . . Paul's list goes on. If your relationships have Jesus as Lord, then they should have these qualities. If they don't, there's a big room you've locked Him out of.

Lord of My Work

Is there a dichotomy between what goes on in your life on Sunday and what goes on during the rest of the week? Is Jesus Lord of your work as well as your Sabbath?

> There is one body and one Spirit, just as also you were called in one hope of your calling. . . . And

He gave some as apostles, and some as prophets, and some as evangelists, and some as pastors and teachers. (Eph. 4:4, 11)

A vocation is literally a calling. Often, God calls us into certain fields of service by giving us specific gifts. Just as He gifted some to be apostles, so He gifted others to be artists. Some to be prophets, others to be physicians. Some, evangelists; others, electricians. Some, pastors and teachers; others, postal workers and therapists. If He's not Lord Monday through Saturday, there's little good in making Him King for a day on Sunday, is there?

Lord of My Circumstances

Ephesians 4:14–15 reveals another external the Lord should control—our attitude toward our circumstances.

As a result, we are no longer to be children, tossed here and there by waves, and carried about by every wind of doctrine, by the trickery of men, by craftiness in deceitful scheming; but speaking the truth in love, we are to grow up in all aspects into Him, who is the head, even Christ.

Tossed about by waves? Up one moment, down another? Dry one second, drenched the next? That's the way children are. Happy when they get their way, moody when they don't. They are gullible, willing to trust no matter what, just wanting to be kept comfortable. This is proper and precious in a child—but not in an adult.

If Jesus is Lord of your circumstances, you will find—in the midst of your stormy seas—a growing stability that is shaken less and less by moods and the desire to have your own way. Instead of seeking comfort at any cost, you will want to please Christ; for you'll know that He who rules the wind and the waves also rules your circumstances.

Lord of My Body

The Church is the body of Christ. When all the members grow up and leave their childish habits and pettiness behind, the body matures and develops, functioning like a well-oiled machine.

From whom the whole body, being fitted and held together by that which every joint supplies, according to the proper working of each individual part,

causes the growth of the body for the building up of
itself in love. (v. 16)

God's concern for the body, however, doesn't stop with the
Church—the spiritual body; it extends to our physical bodies as
well. After all, if our bodies are the temple of the Holy Spirit,
shouldn't He be concerned if the temple is about to cave in or be
condemned (see 1 Cor. 3:16–17; 2 Cor. 6:14–18)?

How about that temple? Is the kitchen your house of worship?
Is the refrigerator the cubical Buddha that satisfies all your inner
cravings? What about the bedroom? Is your bed the altar upon
which your morality and integrity are sacrificed?

From fattening foods to stolen sex, the body can be a traitor
when Jesus isn't enthroned in your life. If the Holy Spirit resides in
you, don't you want Him to live in a temple of marble rather than
of mud and mire? If so, then your body is what has to go on the altar.

I urge you therefore, brethren, by the mercies of
God, to present your bodies a living and holy sacrifice, acceptable to God, which is your spiritual service of worship. And do not be conformed to this
world, but be transformed by the renewing of your
mind, that you may prove what the will of God is,
that which is good and acceptable and perfect.
(Rom. 12:1–2)

Jesus: Lord of All My Internals

Getting a grip on the externals is sometimes slippery business—
like a three-year-old trying to take hold of a bar of soap in the
bathtub. Oddly enough, though, three-year-olds do manage to corral
a bar of Ivory now and again. The key to *consistently* managing this
elusive task, however, simply comes with maturity.

When we grow older, soap is so much easier to handle. The
same is true in coming to grips with the lordship of Jesus over the
external things in our lives. As we mature internally, we seem to
grasp the externals rather naturally. So the real key to having Jesus
as master of your externals is to first enthrone Him over your
internals—your mind, emotions, and will.

Lord of My Mind

In the second half of Ephesians 4, Paul stresses the importance of Jesus being Lord of the mind.

> This I say therefore, and affirm together with the Lord, that you walk no longer just as the Gentiles also walk, in the futility of their mind, being darkened in their understanding, excluded from the life of God, because of the ignorance that is in them, because of the hardness of their heart; and they, having become callous, have given themselves over to sensuality, for the practice of every kind of impurity with greediness. (vv. 17–19)

Notice the harsh terms Paul uses to describe a person rebelling against Christ: *futile, darkened, excluded, ignorant, hard, calloused, given over to sensuality, impure, greedy.*

When Christ's reign is welcomed, though, *renewed, righteous, holy,* and *true* are the defining adjectives.

> But you did not learn Christ in this way, if indeed you have heard Him and have been taught in Him, just as truth is in Jesus, that, in reference to your former manner of life, you lay aside the old self, which is being corrupted in accordance with the lusts of deceit, and that you be renewed in the spirit of your mind, and put on the new self, which in the likeness of God has been created in righteousness and holiness of the truth. (vv. 20–24)

Like a filthy shirt reeking with sweat, stained with blood, and saturated with grime, our old selves are to be laid aside and dropped into the trash. And with a renewed mind that is showered and clean, we are to put on the fresh, pure garments of the new self.

Lord of My Emotions

In verses 25–29, Paul specifically tells how the decision to lay aside the old self and put on the new affects every area of our lives—including our emotions.

> Therefore, laying aside falsehood, speak truth, each one of you, with his neighbor, for we are members of one another. Be angry, and yet do not sin; do not let the sun go down on your anger, and do not give the devil an opportunity. Let him who steals

steal no longer; but rather let him labor, performing with his own hands what is good, in order that he may have something to share with him who has need. Let no unwholesome word proceed from your mouth, but only such a word as is good for edification according to the need of the moment, that it may give grace to those who hear.

If we're not careful, our emotions can take us hostage. Notice the four terrorists Paul unmasks: falsehood (v. 25), anger (v. 26), theft (v. 28), and unwholesome speech (v. 29). Each is ruthless and without scruples. Each, a killer, able to assassinate our character and torch our testimony.

Our emotions say "I'm cornered, so it's OK to lie," or "I'm staying angry until she apologizes," or "It's not really stealing; I've got it coming to me," or "So-and-so needed telling off, and besides, everybody talks that way." But if Jesus is Lord of our emotions, these victimizing feelings should be met with swift and certain justice. "I must tell the truth, even when I feel that it's in my best interest to lie." "I must control my temper, even when I feel enraged or wronged." "I must work hard to provide for myself and others, even when the easy but dishonest buck entices me." "I must muzzle my mouth when it comes to filthy or defamatory talk, and I must train my tongue to lick wounds, not inflict them—even when I've been bitten first."

Lord of My Will

In verses 30–32, Paul calls on our will to take decisive action.

And do not grieve the Holy Spirit of God, by whom you were sealed for the day of redemption. Let all bitterness and wrath and anger and clamor and slander be put away from you, along with all malice. And be kind to one another, tender-hearted, forgiving each other, just as God in Christ also has forgiven you.

In verse 30, the construction of the Greek verb helps make a dramatic point: "Stop it! Stop grieving the Holy Spirit!" Here Paul brings us to the crossroads of decision. Are you for Christ or against Him? Whose side are you really on? There's no middle road. No fence to straddle. Ultimately, the whole lordship question boils down to a decision of the will. Are you going to lay aside the old self and enthrone Jesus as Lord—or are you going to continue to walk around in filthy, smelly rags?

A Concluding Thought

Robert Munger's excellent little book *My Heart—Christ's Home* takes us on a creative but convicting tour of a man's heart, which is described using the imagery of a home. He takes Christ, who has come into his heart, on a brief and self-conscious walk-through. He takes Him through the study, where the mind resides; into the dining room, where the appetites and desires dine; into the living room, where his relationship with Christ was to be deepened and cultivated; into the workroom, where his talents and skills find their outlet; into the recreation room, where certain questionable associations and activities are entertained; into the bedroom, where the issues of sex and love rest.

Room by room, Jesus beautifully transforms the home. But one day, Jesus notices a stench coming from the hall closet. Some rotting remnant of the man's old life was hidden there—something he was ashamed of but didn't want to part with. Do you have a closet like that? As shameful as it may be, let Jesus in to clean it up. Let His sunshine and fresh air take away the smell. And give the King a castle that is worthy of His presence.[1]

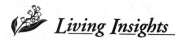 *Living Insights*   STUDY ONE

Is your heart Christ's home? Have you given Him the keys to every room and handed Him the title deed? Or are certain places off-limits, restricted from the prying eyes of nosy guests?

In this chapter, we walked through four external areas—relationships, work, circumstances, and body—which we'll cover in this study; and three internal areas—mind, emotions, and will—which we'll examine in Study Two. Have you hung a Do Not Disturb sign over any of these?

Let's look at each room in more detail and see if Christ is truly Lord of it or if He's been told to stay in the guest house out back.

1. See Robert Munger's *My Heart—Christ's Home*, 2d. rev. ed. (Downers Grove, Ill.: Inter-Varsity Press, 1992).

Relationships

Are your relationships thriving on humility, gentleness, patience, forbearance, love, diligence, unity, and peace (Eph. 4:2–3)? How would you characterize the way you relate to others?

What does this reveal to you about Christ's lordship?

In what ways can you let Christ strengthen or change this area? In your speech? Attitude? The way you handle disagreement or conflict?

Work

Do you regard your Monday-through-Saturday work as important a calling as Sunday worship (vv. 4, 11)? How well do God's principles define your work ethic? In this room, be sure to look at the closets of honesty; treating your employees with dignity; and performing your duties with diligence, faithfulness, and excellence.

Is Christ Lord of this room?

If He isn't, what does He need to change—and are you willing?

Circumstances

When troubling circumstances come your way, do you respond with a stabilizing faith in the true love of Christ and a desire to grow in Him (v. 15)? Or do you fall prey to fantasized or falsely magnified fears and seek escapist comfort (v. 14)? What goes on in this room of your heart?

_____

_____

_____

Have you let Jesus be the Master here?

_____

How can Christ help you remodel this room?

_____

_____

_____

Your Body

Is your body a temple for God, to be filled with His presence, love, and glory? Or is it used to serve other gods, such as sexual satisfaction, a gluttonous appetite, the highs of drugs and alcohol? How well do God's purposes and your purposes for your body match?

_____

_____

_____

Does Christ preside in this temple?

_____

What do you and Jesus need to change?

_____

_____

_____

Let's continue our tour of your heart's home by peering closely
into the three internal rooms.

Your Mind

When it comes to the way you think, are you teachable and
committed to the righteousness and holiness of truth (Eph. 4:23–24)?
Or do your thoughts like to wander around dark alleys and thrill to
forbidden sensuality (vv. 18–19)? On what do you nourish your mind?

_____

_____

_____

Is Christ enthroned here?

_____

How can you cooperate more fully with Jesus' renewal of your
mind?

_____

_____

_____

Your Emotions

Do your emotions ever urge you to lie, blast someone with anger,
steal, or degrade others with foul or cutting words (vv. 25–29)? To
what extent do your emotions determine your behavior?

_____

_____

_____

Does Christ reign in this room?

_____

What needs to change for Him to draw near to you here?

_____

_____

_____

Your Will

Is your will pliable and yielding to God's touch? Or is there an inflexible stubbornness that grieves the Holy Spirit (vv. 30–32)? Are you willing or willful? How does your will manifest itself?

_____

_____

_____

Is Jesus Lord of your will?

_____

What would His refurbishing touch bring about in this room?

_____

_____

_____

In many homes, a simple plaque hung in a prominent place can keep a family focused on what really matters in life. Perhaps Paul's words to the Philippians can be the plaque you hang on your heart as we close our study of Jesus, our Lord.

> God highly exalted Him, and bestowed on Him the
> name which is above every name, that at the name

of Jesus every knee should bow, of those who are in heaven, and on earth, and under the earth, and that every tongue should confess that Jesus Christ is Lord, to the glory of God the Father. (Phil. 2:9–11)

A TIME FOR REFLECTION

This brief but exhilarating journey with Christ has taken us from the deep mystery of His preexistence to His incarnate presence on the earth, from the terrors of the Cross to the sweet relief of the empty tomb, from His throne in heaven to His throne in each of our hearts.

What has meant the most to you in this study? What have you learned about our Lord that you didn't know before? How have you grown closer to Him? Before rushing on to your next Bible study, linger awhile longer in His presence, won't you? Ponder those questions, and write down any changes you've felt prompted to make in your life based on these glimpses of Jesus.

May others see Christ more clearly in you as a result of the time you spend with Him.

Jesus, Our Lord

Jesus: His Existence before Creation _____

_____

_____

Jesus: A Birth like None Other _____

_____

_____

Jesus: His God-Man Lifestyle _____

_____

_____

Jesus: A Lamb Led to Slaughter _____

_____

_____

Jesus: Triumphant over the Grave _____

_____

_____

Jesus: Ascended and Seated in Heaven _____

_____

_____

Jesus: His Promised Return _____

_____

_____

Jesus: He Is Lord _____

_____

_____

——————◆——————

No distant Lord have I,
    Loving afar to be.
Made flesh for me He cannot rest
    Until He rests in me. . . .

Ascended now to God
    My witness there to be,
His witness here am I because
    His Spirit dwells in me.[1]

1. Maltbie D. Babcock, "No Distant Lord," in *Masterpieces of Religious Verse*, ed. James Dalton Morrison (New York, N.Y.: Harper and Brothers Publishers, 1948), p. 254.

BOOKS FOR
PROBING FURTHER

Following Jesus as Lord is like a child following his father's footsteps through the heavy snow. The little boy is not left to brave the snowstorm alone. But neither does the father spare the child the cold journey—fighting the elements himself while the child warms his hands by the fireplace at home. Rather, the two go through the snow together. As the father leads, the child sees the example and follows the deep footprints that chart a path through the drifts—one step at a time.

Following Jesus as Lord doesn't melt the snow. It doesn't mean instant spring, with sunshine and flowers. The snow will be just as cold; the drifts, just as deep; the blizzards, just as blinding.

But one important thing does change. Where there was a pathless blanket of freezing snow, there now are footprints pressed deep in the drifts before us—and a warm hand outstretched to keep us from slipping.

I hope these studies have encouraged you to take that first step of making Jesus not only your Savior but also your Lord.

The following books should help you along that journey, training your eyes to look not just at the deep drifts of snow but also at the deep footprints of Christ. And they should also help you follow Him—one step at a time.

Anderson, Norman. *Jesus Christ: The Witness of History*. Downers Grove, Ill.: InterVarsity Press, 1985. Former director of Advanced Legal Studies at the University of London, the author examines the historical evidences of Christ's life with all the rigorous logic and proofs you would expect from a tenacious trial lawyer.

Bruce, F. F. *Jesus: Lord and Savior*. Downers Grove, Ill.: InterVarsity Press, 1986. In fascinating detail, this noted New Testament scholar examines the biblical evidence that answers the question, Who is Jesus? In doing so, he considers Jesus from His preexistence to His Second Coming.

Green, Michael. *The Empty Cross of Jesus*. Downers Grove, Ill.:

InterVarsity Press, 1984. This excellent book examines why Jesus had to die and answers commonly raised objections concerning the Crucifixion and Resurrection.

Griffiths, Michael. *The Example of Jesus.* Downers Grove, Ill.: InterVarsity Press, 1985. Like metal to a magnet, people were drawn to Jesus. Naturally, those who came to know Him wanted to follow His example. The author probes to find out why—and how we, too, can follow the example of Christ.

Lewis, C. S. *Mere Christianity.* Revised and enlarged. 1952. Reprint. New York, N.Y.: Macmillan Publishing Co., 1960. A classic philosophical treatise on the basics of faith in Christ, this helpful book is filled with vivid examples, irrefutable logic, and crackling wit.

Lucado, Max. *God Came Near: Chronicles of the Christ.* Portland, Oreg.: Multnomah Press, 1987. Sensitive and stirring, this book chronicles Christ from His birth in Bethlehem to His life in each of us. Lucado cracks open the dry shell of theology to reveal the vibrant God who wants to be near to us.

————. *No Wonder They Call Him the Savior.* Portland, Oreg.: Multnomah Press, 1986. A book of rare insight, this collection of devotional vignettes plumbs the emotional depths of the Cross. You will never look at the Savior's agony quite the same after having been touched by this tender book.

Munger, Robert Boyd. *My Heart—Christ's Home.* 2d revised edition. Downers Grove, Ill.: InterVarsity Press, 1992. This small, best-selling book examines the lordship of Christ in an extended metaphor—seeing our hearts as homes for Jesus to dwell in and redesign.

Pentecost, J. Dwight. *The Words and Works of Jesus Christ.* Grand Rapids, Mich.: Zondervan Publishing House, Academie Books, 1981. This masterpiece chronologically harmonizes the gospel accounts of the life of Christ and integrates illuminating support from a variety of historical sources.

White, John. *Magnificent Obsession.* Revised edition. Downers Grove, Ill.: InterVarsity Press, 1990. This short but powerful book reveals the practical costs of making Jesus Lord of our lives and shows how those costs pale in light of the surpassing glory of living for the Savior. (Formerly titled *The Cost of Commitment.*)

Some of these books may be out of print and available only through a library. For those currently available, please contact your local Christian bookstore. Books by Charles R. Swindoll may be obtained through Insight for Living. IFL also offers some books by other authors—please note the ordering information that follows and contact the office that serves you.

ORDERING INFORMATION

JESUS, OUR LORD
Cassette Tapes and Study Guide

This Bible study guide was designed to be used independently or in conjunction with the broadcast of Chuck Swindoll's taped messages which are listed below. If you would like to order cassette tapes or further copies of this study guide, please see the information given below and the order form provided at the end of this guide.

		U.S.	Canada
JOL	Study guide	$ 3.95 ea.	$ 5.25 ea.
JOLCS	Cassette series, includes all individual tapes, album cover, and one complimentary study guide	29.20	36.75 ea.
JOL 1–4	Individual cassettes, includes messages A and B	6.30 ea.	8.00 ea.

The prices are subject to change without notice.

JOL   1-A: *Jesus: His Existence before Creation*—Selected Scriptures
    B: *Jesus: A Birth like None Other*—Luke 1:26–35; Matthew 1:18–25

JOL   2-A: *Jesus: His God-Man Lifestyle*—Selected Scriptures
    B: *Jesus: A Lamb Led to Slaughter*—Isaiah 53:1–7; Selected Scriptures

JOL   3-A: *Jesus: Triumphant over the Grave*—John 19:30–20:29
    B: *Jesus: Ascended and Seated in Heaven*—Acts 1:6–11; Ephesians 1:18–23

JOL   4-A: *Jesus: His Promised Return*—Selected Scriptures
    B: *Jesus: He Is Lord*—Ephesians 3:14–4:32

How to Order by Phone or FAX
(Credit card orders only)

United States: 1-800-772-8888 from 7:00 A.M. to 4:30 P.M., Pacific time, Monday through Friday
FAX (714) 575-5496 anytime, day or night

Canada: 1-800-663-7639, Vancouver residents call (604) 596-2910 from
7:00 A.M. to 5:00 P.M., Pacific time, Monday through Friday
FAX (604) 596-2975 anytime, day or night

Australia: (03) 872-4606 or FAX (03) 874-8890 from 9:00 A.M. to
5:00 P.M., Monday through Friday

Other International Locations: call the Ordering Services Department
in the United States at (714) 575-5000 during the hours listed above.

How to Order by Mail

United States
- Mail to: Ordering Services Department
  Insight for Living
  Post Office Box 69000
  Anaheim, CA 92817-0900
- Sales tax: California residents add 7.25%.
- Shipping: add 10% of the total order amount for first-class delivery.
(Otherwise, allow four to six weeks for fourth-class delivery.)
- Payment: personal checks, money orders, credit cards (Visa, Master-
Card, Discover Card, and American Express). No invoices or COD orders
available.
- $10 fee for *any* returned check.

Canada
- Mail to: Insight for Living Ministries
  Post Office Box 2510
  Vancouver, BC V6B 3W7
- Sales tax: please add 7% GST. British Columbia residents also add 7%
sales tax (on tapes or cassette series).
- Shipping: included in prices listed above.
- Payment: personal checks, money orders, credit cards (Visa, Master-
Card). No invoices or COD orders available.
- Delivery: approximately four weeks.

Australia, New Zealand, or Papua New Guinea
- Mail to: Insight for Living, Inc.
  GPO Box 2823 EE
  Melbourne, Victoria 3001, Australia
- Shipping and delivery time: please see chart that follows.

- Payment: personal checks payable in U.S. funds, international money orders, or credit cards (Visa, MasterCard).

Other International Locations
- Mail to: Ordering Services Department
  Insight for Living
  Post Office Box 69000
  Anaheim, CA 92817-0900
- Shipping and delivery time: please see chart that follows.
- Payment: personal checks payable in U.S. funds, international money orders, or credit cards (Visa, MasterCard, and American Express).

Type of Shipping	Postage Cost	Delivery
Surface	10% of total order*	6 to 10 weeks
Airmail	25% of total order*	under 6 weeks

Use U.S. price as a base.

Our Guarantee

Your complete satisfaction is our top priority here at Insight for Living. If you're not completely satisfied with anything you order, please return it for full credit, a refund, or a replacement, as you prefer.

Insight for Living Catalog

The Insight for Living catalog features study guides, tapes, and books by a variety of Christian authors. To obtain a free copy, call us at the numbers listed above.

Order Form
United States, Australia, and Other International Locations
(Canadian residents please use order form on reverse side.)

JOLCS represents the entire *Jesus Our Lord* series in a special album cover, while JOL 1–4 are the individual tapes included in the series. JOL represents this study guide, should you desire to order additional copies.

JOL	Study guide	$ 3.95 ea.
JOLCS	Cassette series, includes all individual tapes, album cover, and one complimentary study guide	29.20
JOL 1–4	Individual cassettes, includes messages A and B	6.30 ea.

Product Code	Product Description	Quantity	Unit Price	Total
			$	$
		Subtotal		
		California Residents—Sales Tax *Add 7.25% of subtotal.*		
		U.S. First-Class Shipping *For faster delivery, add 10% for postage and handling.*		
		Non-United States Residents *U.S. price plus 10% surface postage or 25% airmail.*		
		Gift to Insight for Living *Tax-deductible in the United States.*		
		Total Amount Due *Please do not send cash.*	$	

Prices are subject to change without notice.

Payment by: ❑ Check or money order payable to Insight for Living   ❑ Credit card

(Circle one):   Visa   MasterCard   Discover Card   American Express

Number _____

Expiration Date _____   Signature _____

We cannot process your credit card purchase without your signature.

Name _____

Address _____

City _____   State _____

Zip Code _____   Country _____

Telephone (___) _____   Radio Station ____ ____ ____ ____

If questions arise concerning your order, we may need to contact you.

Mail this order form to the Ordering Services Department at one of these addresses:

Insight for Living
Post Office Box 69000, Anaheim, CA 92817-0900

Insight for Living, Inc.
GPO Box 2823 EE, Melbourne, VIC 3001, Australia

ECFA
MEMBER

Order Form
Canadian Residents
(Residents of the United States, Australia, and other international locations, please use order form on reverse side.)

JOLCS represents the entire *Jesus Our Lord* series in a special album cover, while JOL 1–4 are the individual tapes included in the series. JOL represents this study guide, should you desire to order additional copies.

JOL	Study guide	$ 5.25 ea.
JOLCS	Cassette series,	36.75
	includes all individual tapes, album cover, and one complimentary study guide	
JOL 1–4	Individual cassettes,	8.00 ea.
	includes messages A and B	

Product Code	Product Description	Quantity	Unit Price	Total
			$	$
		Subtotal		
		Add 7% GST		
		British Columbia Residents *Add 7% sales tax on individual tapes or cassette series.*		
		Gift to Insight for Living Ministries *Tax-deductible in Canada.*		
		Total Amount Due *Please do not send cash.*	$	

Prices are subject to change without notice.

Payment by: ❑ Check or money order payable to Insight for Living Ministries
❑ Credit card

(Circle one): Visa   MasterCard   Number _____

Expiration Date _____   Signature _____
We cannot process your credit card purchase without your signature.

Name _____

Address _____

City _____ Province _____

Postal Code _____ Country _____

Telephone ( ) _____ Radio Station ____ ____ ____ ____
If questions arise concerning your order, we may need to contact you.

Mail this order form to the Ordering Services Department at the following address:

Insight for Living Ministries
Post Office Box 2510
Vancouver, BC, Canada V6B 3W7